Lives in Limbo

LIVES IN LIMBO

Refugee Place-Making and Survival in Malaysia

Gerhard Hoffstaedter

Stanford
Walter H. Shorenstein
Asia-Pacific Research Center
Freeman Spogli Institute

Shorenstein APARC addresses critical issues affecting the countries of Asia, their regional and global affairs, and U.S.-Asia relations. As Stanford University's hub for the interdisciplinary study of contemporary Asia, we produce policy-relevant research, provide education and training to students, scholars, and practitioners, and strengthen dialogue and cooperation between counterparts in the Asia-Pacific and the United States.

Walter H. Shorenstein Asia-Pacific Research Center
Stanford University
616 Jane Stanford Way, Encina Hall
Stanford, CA 94305-6055
650-723-9741 | aparc.fsi.stanford.edu

Published by the Walter H. Shorenstein Asia-Pacific Research Center

Distributed by Stanford University Press

Library of Congress Cataloging-in-Publication data is available

ISBN 978-1-931368-76-6 (paper)
ISBN 978-1-931368-77-3 (eBook)

For Nicole

CONTENTS

LIST OF FIGURES

GLOSSARY AND ABBREVIATIONS

3D JOBS Dirty, dangerous, and demeaning work that refugees often perform in Malaysia's informal economy.

ABIM Angkatan Belia Islam Malaysia (Muslim Youth Movement of Malaysia)

ACR Alliance for Chin Refugees, a refugee community organization providing health and other services.

ARAKANESE/RAKHINE The Buddhist ethnic majority in Rakhine State, Myanmar, from where Rohingya also originate.

ARRC Arakan Refugee Relief Committee, representing Rakhine refugees in Malaysia.

ASEAN Association of Southeast Asian Nations, a regional intergovernmental organization comprising eleven member states in Southeast Asia.

ASYLUM ACCESS An international legal NGO providing support to refugees in status determination processes.

BAMAR The ethnic majority group in Myanmar, also known as Burmese.

BATU ARANG A town northwest of Kuala Lumpur, historically a coal mining area, now home to refugee farming communities.

BETEL LEAVES Leaves from the betel vine, chewed with areca nut, popular among people from Myanmar and grown on refugee farms.

BUMIPUTERA Literally "sons of the soil" in Malay; refers to the Indigenous peoples of Malaysia, primarily Malays and Indigenous groups from East Malaysia, who receive constitutional privileges.

CAMERON HIGHLANDS A hill station in Malaysia where approximately 3,000 Chin refugees work in farms.

CNF Chin National Front, an ethnic armed organization in Myanmar's Chin State.

COBEM Coalition of Burma Ethnics Malaysia, an umbrella organization representing ethnic refugee organizations from Myanmar.

CONIFA Confederation of Independent Football Associations, an international football organization for teams from stateless peoples, minorities, and unrecognized states.

CRC Chin Refugee Committee, one of the largest refugee community organizations in Malaysia.

EID AL-FITR Islamic festival marking the end of Ramadan.

HAKHA Capital of and the largest township in Chin State, Myanmar.

HALAL Food prepared according to Islamic law.

HINDRAF Hindu Rights Action Force, which filed a class action suit challenging Malaysia's social contract.

IMM13 A temporary immigration document that Malaysia issued to certain refugee groups, such as Acehnese refugees in the early 2000s.

JATROPHA A cash crop that Myanmar military forces farmers to grow, replacing traditional food crops.

KACHIN An ethnic minority from northern Myanmar, predominantly Christian.

KAREN An ethnic minority from eastern Myanmar, many living in refugee camps in Thailand.

KARENNI An ethnic minority from Kayah State, eastern Myanmar.

KELANTAN A state in peninsular Malaysia with a large Malay Muslim population.

KLANG VALLEY The urban conglomeration around Kuala Lumpur where most refugees in Malaysia reside.

KRC Kachin Refugee Committee, representing Kachin refugees in Malaysia.

MADRASAH Islamic religious school providing religious education alongside basic literacy and numeracy.

MCA Malaysian Chinese Association.

MIC Malaysian Indian Congress.

MKO Malaysia Karen Organization, representing Karen refugees.

MON An ethnic minority from Mon State in southern Myanmar.

MRAUK U Ancient capital of the Arakan kingdom in present-day Rakhine State.

MRO Mon Refugee Organization, representing Mon refugees in Malaysia.

MUEZZIN The person who calls Muslims to prayer from a mosque.

MUFTI A senior Islamic scholar qualified to issue religious rulings.

NEP New Economic Policy, Malaysia's affirmative action program for Bumiputera implemented after 1969.

OIC Organization of Islamic Cooperation, of which Malaysia is a member.

OKD Organization of Karenni Development, representing Karenni refugees.

ORANG ASLI Indigenous peoples of peninsular Malaysia.

PAHANG A state in peninsular Malaysia.

PAK CIK Respectful term for an older man in Malay, literally "uncle."

PAS Parti Islam Se-Malaysia, Malaysia's main Islamic political party.

PENDATANG Literally "newcomer" in Malay; often used pejoratively to describe non-Malay Malaysians and foreign migrants.

POLYCRISIS The multiplicity and cascading effects of multiple, interconnected crises that compound vulnerability.

RAMADAN The Islamic month of fasting, when charitable giving to refugees increases.

RELA Ikatan Relawan Rakyat Malaysia (People's Volunteer Corps), a volunteer civilian auxiliary force that assists with immigration enforcement.

RFC Rohingya Football Club, a refugee community organization using sport for identity maintenance.

RINGGIT MALAYSIA (RM) Malaysian currency.

SELAYANG An area north of Kuala Lumpur with high refugee concentrations, particularly Rohingya and Myanmar Muslims.

SHAN An ethnic minority from Shan State in eastern Myanmar.

SITTWE Capital city of Rakhine State, Myanmar.

SRO Shan Refugee Organization, representing Shan refugees in Malaysia.

SUARAM Suara Rakyat Malaysia (Voice of the Malaysian People), a human rights organization.

SWIDDEN AGRICULTURE Slash-and-burn farming traditionally practiced in the Chin Hills.

TEMPORARY AUTONOMOUS ZONES (TAZ) Spaces where alternative forms of social organization can emerge outside state control, adapted here to describe refugee community activities.

TENAGANITA A Malaysian NGO advocating for migrant and refugee rights.

UMNO United Malays National Organization, formerly Malaysia's dominant political party.

UNHCR United Nations High Commissioner for Refugees, the UN agency mandated to protect and assist refugees worldwide.

UNRWA United Nations Relief and Works Agency for Palestine Refugees in the Near East.

USTAZ An Islamic religious teacher or scholar.

YANGON Largest city and former capital of Myanmar.

ZAKAT One of the five pillars of Islam requiring Muslims to give portions of their wealth to the poor and needy.

ZOMI An ethnic identity claimed by some Chin peoples, meaning "hill people" in their language. The term represents resistance to the colonial designation "Chin."

ACKNOWLEDGMENTS

This book has been a long journey in the making, beginning with a short fieldwork trip in 2009 to stay with my friend, Fr. Aloysius Mowe, a Jesuit priest and one of those encyclopedic scholars the academy no longer produces. He had studied at Al-Azhar and Oxford and was a specialist in the history of Islam, but really a master narrator on any topic. I had studied Islam in Malaysia for my PhD, and during fieldwork bumped into him to discuss interreligious dialogue in Malaysia. My interlocutors had often taken me around town, where we would interact with people they dismissed as "foreigners," serving tea at the local mamak stalls, washing cars, and cleaning the streets, and I was intent on finding out more. When I visited Aloysius, he immediately recognized that they were most likely refugees from Myanmar, and said he could introduce me to some people, as the Jesuits had been active in supporting refugees in Malaysia. The next day, I was sitting in the offices of a health clinic run by A Call to Serve (ACTS), waiting to talk to a doctor. Next to me was a young Chin man from Myanmar, and we began to chat about this and that. Upon hearing that I was interested in learning more about refugees, he took me under his wing and introduced me to refugees and organizations over the next two weeks. Meeting Simon that day changed my trajectory as he swept me up in the messy politics of Malaysia, the country's amazing people, the food, and the lives refugees were making there while living in legal limbo. Ours turned out to be an enduring friendship, and I am glad he is now resettled in Australia with his family. It planted in me the seeds to pursue the lives of refugees in Malaysia for the last seventeen years and write this book to help make sense of it all.

Thus, my acknowledgments are far and wide, spanning time and space, from Malaysia to Australia and Myanmar, from 2009 to the present. First and foremost, I want to acknowledge and thank the hundreds of refugees who have taken me in and have been gracious enough to allow me to accompany them, sit with them, and hear their remarkable stories. You will read many of them throughout the book, but there are so many other stories, not mine to tell, not within the remit of the book, or just too wild and unbelievable to tell now. Refugees from the Rohingya, Chin, Zomi, Karen, Kachin, Karenni, Mon, Shan, Burmese, Rakhine, Sudanese, Somali, Tamil, and Afghan communities have shared their lives with me. Here, a special mention to the many kind people at the Chin Refugee Committee, with whom I stayed and have accompanied ever since, and the community in Batu Arang, who took me in. Malaysian and expat supporters and interested parties, above all Sarah Devaraj, as well as staff from a range of service providers, NGOs, and the UNHCR, have contributed their valuable insights over the years.

My thanks extend to academic companions, readers, critics, and supporters, especially Aslam Abd Jalil and Antje Missbach, who have engaged with this work in its various forms. To the community research assistants Jack, Kabir, Sabath, Suu, Anwar, Sharifah, and Australia-based research assistant Jennifer Rowe, who helped make the fieldwork possible. To wayfarers in the field and beyond, Mahen Bala and James Rose, who accompanied me along the way. I also appreciated readers of parts of the book, including Ghassan Hage, Gillian Tan, Michael Jackson, John Cash, and Sverre Molland. I presented varying parts of the book at seminars and conferences at universities in Singapore, Malaysia, the United States, Australia, Germany, and the United Kingdom, and received valuable feedback, but all shortcomings remain my own.

I was also the thankful recipient of an Australian Research Council Discovery Early Career Research Award that allowed me to spend twelve months in the field and the Lee Kong Chian NUS-Stanford fellowship on contemporary Southeast Asia that made the writing of the book possible, as well as sabbaticals from my home institution, the University of Queensland. My thanks to Don Emmerson for his support, Tom Fingar's readership, and George Krompacky Jr.'s excellent management of the publication process at Stanford University's Shorenstein Asia-Pacific Research Center.

None of this, nor I, would be in the position to write, let alone publish a book, without the unwavering support of Dr. Nicole Lamb, my partner in the truest sense of the word, who quit her job to accompany me into the field and interview, talk to, travel with, and work with refugees. It has taken longer than anticipated, and two children later, it is finally finished. Thank you. It is to her I dedicate this book.

All photographs are mine.

Lives in Limbo

INTRODUCTION

Place-making in the Polycrisis

Rahman,[1] a 20-year-old Rohingya man, worked at a wet market in Kuala Lumpur, portering heavy boxes of produce and minding the stall for his Chinese Malaysian boss. The work was physically demanding but reliable. Each morning, Rahman would arrive before dawn to help his boss set up the stall, arranging fresh vegetables and fruits that had been trucked in from farms across Malaysia. He would spend his days lifting heavy crates, sorting produce, serving customers, and keeping the stall organized. Despite the hard labor and long hours, the job provided him with a steady income that allowed him to look after his family, send remittances back to his family in a refugee camp in Bangladesh, and maintain hope for his future. Then, rumors of a new virus swept through the market.

When the COVID-19 restrictions and lockdowns began in Malaysia, refugees like Rahman lost their jobs almost immediately. Unlike Malaysian citizens or legal residents who might have access to government support or unemployment benefits, Rahman and thousands of other refugees found themselves completely cut off from any safety net. Without any legal status, they received no help from the government. On the contrary, they became vilified as potential harborers of the virus, and their bodies were subjected to ever-tighter surveillance (Jalil and Hoffstaedter 2023). The media and public discourse increasingly portrayed refugees and migrant communities as dis-

1 All names have been anonymized in order to protect refugee and participant identities.

ease vectors, responsible for spreading the contagion. What had once been a relationship of mutual dependence between refugees providing cheap labor and employers benefiting from their work suddenly transformed into suspicion and blame.

The police and military were brought in to physically close off migrant and refugee neighborhoods for fear their movements would spread the virus. Entire communities were cordoned off, with security forces preventing residents from leaving their immediate areas (Jalil and Hoffstaedter 2023). These closures were not based on actual infection rates or medical evidence, but rather on assumptions about hygiene and health practices in refugee communities. The restrictions meant that even those refugees who might have found alternative work were now physically prevented from seeking employment. Without a way to earn money, Rahman had to plead with his community and friends to help source funds to feed his family. The informal networks of mutual support that had always been crucial to refugee survival became even more vital during the pandemic. Community members shared what little they had, religious organizations provided food assistance where possible, and families stretched their savings to help neighbors. But these networks were themselves under strain, as nearly everyone in the community faced the same predicament.

This was not the future he had imagined for himself and his family when he boarded a rickety boat for a treacherous journey across the Andaman Sea three years ago. Like many Rohingya before him, Rahman had risked everything on the dangerous sea crossing from Myanmar to Malaysia, driven by persecution and the promise of a better life. The journey itself was harrowing, with overcrowded boats, the threat of capsizing, and the constant risk of being intercepted by traffickers or hostile authorities. But Rahman had endured it all with the hope that Malaysia, as a Muslim-majority country, would offer sanctuary and opportunity. He had heard stories from other Rohingya about finding work and earning decent wages; eventually, perhaps even being resettled to a safe third country was a possibility, one where his children could have a proper education and legal status. The wet market job, despite its difficulties, had represented progress toward that dream. Now, confined to his neighborhood and unable to work, watching his community being blamed for a global pandemic, Rahman found himself questioning whether the dangerous journey had been worth it. The COVID-19 crisis stripped away the thin veneer of tolerance that had allowed refugees to exist on the margins of Malaysian society, revealing the fundamental precariousness of their position as people without legal status or rights in a country that had never officially recognized their presence.

Rahman's story during the COVID-19 pandemic crystallizes the central questions that drive this book: How do refugees experience life in protracted situations without legal status in countries like Malaysia? What forms of agency do refugees exercise within systems designed to exclude them? How do refugees create meaningful lives and communities despite systematic marginalization? And what can refugee experiences teach us about the nature of belonging, citizenship, and human rights in contemporary Southeast Asia? These questions emerge from a fundamental tension in Malaysia's approach to refugee protection: the simultaneous dependence on refugee labor, especially in the vast informal economy, and rejection of refugee rights. This contradiction creates a "protection paradox," where refugees are economically integrated but socially excluded, practically tolerated but legally prohibited, individually welcomed but collectively rejected.

This book argues that understanding this paradox requires moving beyond traditional approaches that focus either on state policies or refugee experiences in isolation. Instead, it develops a relational analysis that examines how refugee agency and state strategies interact to create complex patterns of exclusion and belonging. This analysis reveals how refugees are not simply victims of circumstances beyond their control but active participants in systems that simultaneously constrain and enable their survival (Nyers 2006). The theoretical framework I develop throughout this study draws on recent scholarship on place-making and urban migration (explored comprehensively in chapter 5), the politics of hospitality and conditional welcome (examined in detail in chapter 2), and the creation of community through cultural practices (analyzed through sporting activities and cultural celebrations in chapter 7). The polycrisis framework proves essential for understanding these dynamics, as I demonstrate particularly in chapter 4's analysis of how refugees navigate multiple intersecting forms of exclusion and marginalization.

Rahman's experience during COVID-19 illustrates how health, economic, legal, and social crises intersect to create effects that are greater than the sum of their parts. The pandemic did not simply add another problem to refugees' existing difficulties; it revealed the fundamental interconnectedness of multiple systems of exclusion and the ways these systems can rapidly intensify refugee vulnerability. Yet the book also reveals how refugees develop strategies for surviving and thriving within these constraints, and how they create forms of belonging that operate alongside, rather than against, their systematic exclusion. These strategies include the development of parallel community institutions, strategic deployment of religious and ethnic identities, creation of informal economic networks, and cultivation of transnational connections that provide both material support and emotional sustenance.

The book's focus on Chin and Rohingya refugees, whose historical trajectories and contemporary experiences I trace in chapter 1, demonstrates how different forms of displacement create different possibilities for agency and belonging. The comparative analysis shows how factors such as religion, education, international advocacy networks, and host-country policies interact in complex ways to shape refugee experiences. It challenges simplistic narratives about refugee integration while revealing the sophisticated ways that refugees navigate systems of exclusion. The ethnographic foundation of this study, based on over twelve months of intensive fieldwork and more than 80 formal interviews, enables a deep analysis of how these processes unfold in practice. The methodological approach, which I detail below, emphasizes long-term engagement and community-based research that positions refugees as active collaborators rather than passive subjects of study.

Ultimately, this book argues that refugee experiences in Malaysia reveal broader truths about the nature of belonging and exclusion in contemporary Southeast Asia. By examining how refugees create meaningful lives despite systematic marginalization, the book contributes to debates about citizenship, human rights, and the possibilities for more inclusive forms of political community. Rahman's story, and the thousands of others like it, challenge us to reimagine what protection, belonging, and human security might mean in our interconnected but deeply unequal world.

REFRAMING THE "CRISIS" NARRATIVE

Whenever we speak about refugees, a crisis narrative continues to dominate the discourse. When states and media outlets speak of a "refugee crisis," they typically invoke images of overwhelming numbers, disorder, and threats to security. However, these narratives obscure a fundamental reality: refugees constitute only a small fraction of the world's population. According to the United Nations High Commissioner for Refugees (UNHCR) and its *Global Trends* report, there were approximately 26 million refugees under the UNHCR's mandate in 2019 out of a global population of 7.7 billion people, representing roughly 0.34 percent of the world's population (UNHCR 2023; UN DESA 2019a). Among the 272 million international migrants worldwide, refugees represent only about 9.5 percent of total international migration (UN DESA 2019b). As migration scholar Hein de Haas has argued, these numbers tell a particular kind of narrative: a crisis story that helps the aid sector secure funding and justifies increasingly restrictive border policies, despite the relatively small scale of refugee movements globally (de Haas 2008, 2023).

Thus, the crisis framing serves specific political purposes. Regional states and the international community often frame large population movements as emergencies to conjure notions of disorder and justify the securitization of mobility, to create stronger border protection mechanisms, and even to close borders. This leads to policies focused on containment and deterrence rather than protection. The unidimensional crisis that many states describe, usually through the arrival of large numbers of refugees, deliberately hides the structural and underlying causes of displacement: systematic persecution, economic inequality, environmental degradation, and the legacies of colonialism. Such crisis narratives place the burden of responsibility on refugees themselves, portraying them as a problem to be solved rather than as people exercising agency in often impossible circumstances (Nyers 2006). Rahman's story illustrates how this framing operates: when COVID-19 emerged, refugees were quickly scapegoated as disease vectors rather than recognized as frontline workers who had been integral to Malaysia's economy. The "crisis" was deemed not to be the virus itself, but rather the presence of refugees who might spread it.

To move beyond these limiting narratives, this book employs the concept of *polycrisis*, which denotes the multiplicity and cascading effects of multiple, interconnected crises. First used by French philosopher Edgar Morin and developed by historian Adam Tooze, polycrisis speaks to what Morin and Kern (1999, 74) describe as the "complex intersolidarity of problems, antagonisms, [and] crises" that characterize contemporary global challenges. The polycrisis framework is particularly fitting for understanding refugee displacement in Southeast Asia, where crises are compounded by preexisting structural vulnerabilities. Rahman's experience during COVID-19 exemplifies this: the health crisis intersected with preexisting economic precarity, legal exclusion, and social marginalization to create a situation far more devastating than any single crisis alone. The pandemic did not simply add another problem to refugees' lives; it revealed and intensified the fundamental structural violence of their legal limbo.

In Malaysia's context, the polycrisis includes: the ongoing persecution and displacement from Myanmar; the absence of legal frameworks for refugee protection; the economic dependence on cheap migrant labor; the racialized politics of Malaysian multiculturalism; and the global systems that make Malaysia a transit country rather than a destination for permanent settlement. Each crisis feeds into and amplifies the others, creating what refugees experience as a state of permanent limbo or emergency. This interconnected nature of multiple crises becomes particularly evident in my analysis of how refugees navigate healthcare systems that serve as sites of surveillance rather than care (chapter 5), how they develop agricultural livelihoods that provide both economic security and deeper forms of place-making (chapter 6), and how they encounter conditional forms of hospitality that reflect broader patterns of inclusion and exclusion in Malaysian society (chapter 2).

Importantly, the polycrisis framework shows how transit countries like Malaysia actively deepen these crises through policies that maintain refugees in legal limbo while simultaneously exploiting their labor. This is not accidental but represents a system where refugees' vulnerability becomes economically and politically useful and therefore exploitable by the host state. The polycrisis thus operates not as a series of unfortunate coincidences but as a structured system of marginalization that serves specific interests while maintaining plausible deniability about responsibility. I expand on the concept and its role in Malaysia in chapter 4.

CHIN AND ROHINGYA PEOPLES: CONTESTED IDENTITIES AND COLONIAL LEGACIES

In my many years of accompanying refugees in Malaysia, I quickly realized that the two largest refugee cohorts were the Chin and the Rohingya. The first refugee I encountered in the field was at a medical center where I had gone to interview service providers; he turned out to be Chin and, as it happened, an activist; he took me under his wing to better understand the internal ethnic politics of Myanmar and ultimately the internal ethnic politics of Chin themselves. Both Chin and Rohingya have been fleeing Myanmar for many years, decades even, and both have complicated histories, internally and as opposed to the Bamar majority in Myanmar. Indeed, both ethnic labels remain highly contested, with their contemporary meanings rooted in the complex legacies of British colonialism in Myanmar. These identities were not simply inherited from precolonial societies but were actively constructed through colonial administrative practices, missionary activities, and anti-colonial resistance movements. Understanding these historical formations is crucial for comprehending how these groups experience displacement and seek protection in Malaysia today, as I explore through detailed case studies of contemporary registration processes and the development of community organizations and support networks (examined across multiple chapters).

Chin people represent a linguistically and ethnically diverse collection of hill tribes from the mountainous northwest of Myanmar, traditionally inhabiting the Chin Hills that straddle the borders of Myanmar, India, and Bangladesh (Lehman 1963). What unites these diverse groups today is primarily their shared Christian faith, the result of intensive missionary activity by American Baptist and other Protestant missions beginning in the late nineteenth century (Sakhong 2003). The conversion of formerly animist tribes to Christianity was transformative, creating what scholar Lian Sakhong (2003) describes as a modern, unified Chin identity that transcended traditional tribal boundaries. Christianity provided not only religious beliefs but also educational opportunities, as missions established schools that taught literacy in both Chin languages and English. This educational foundation has had lasting effects, with many Chin refugees arriving in Malaysia possessing higher levels of formal education compared to other refugee groups (Hoffstaedter 2014b), a factor that significantly influences their experiences of place-making and community organization.

Since Myanmar's independence in 1948, the Chin people have faced systematic persecution under successive military governments. This persecution has taken distinctly religious forms: the removal of Christian crosses from public spaces, the harassment and imprisonment of pastors, and the enforcement of Buddhist nationalist policies that marginalize religious minorities (Chin Human Rights Organization 2012b). The military government's "Burmanization" campaign has sought to impose Burmese Buddhist culture on ethnic minorities, viewing Christianity as a foreign influence that threatens national unity (Mang 2011). A 2011 report determined that 92 percent of households in Chin State had been subjected to forced labor, including portering, road building, and growing cash crops for the Myanmar military (Physicians for Human Rights 2011). Many Chin refugees describe fleeing after witnessing the destruction of churches, the persecution of religious leaders, or being forced to participate in Buddhist ceremonies. The religious character of their persecution has important implications for how they seek protection: Chin refugees often emphasize their Christian identity when applying for asylum, and their churches serve as crucial community organizing centers in Malaysia (Hoffstaedter 2014b; Hoffstaedter and Lamb 2019).

The Rohingya people present a more complex and tragic case of displacement. A predominantly Sunni Muslim ethnic minority from Rakhine State in Myanmar, the Rohingya population numbers approximately two million people, with fewer than one million remaining in Myanmar and the majority now living in diaspora communities across Bangladesh, Southeast Asia, and the Middle East (Hoffstaedter 2020). Both Rakhine and Myanmar are Buddhist-majority states, and ethnic and religious tensions have been an ongoing concern, resulting in the displacement of hundreds of thousands of Rohingya over the last century and what have been described as crimes against humanity, ethnic cleansing, and a genocide. Rohingya trace their historical roots in the region to the Arakan kingdom, centered in Mrauk U, which ruled the region from the fifteenth to the eighteenth century. Mrauk U was a Buddhist kingdom heavily influenced by neighboring Islamic sultanates in the Indian subcontinent, especially the neighboring sultanate of Bengal, of which it was, for a while, a vassal state. Before that, Muslim traders from the Arabian Peninsula, Persia, and the Indian subcontinent frequented the region since the eighth or eleventh century; some were said to have been shipwrecked here, others established strong trading outposts, and many settled in the region's ports, bringing with them the religion of Islam.

The colonial period fundamentally transformed regional dynamics. In the late eighteenth century (1784), the Burmese conquered Arakan, and many Muslims fled across the border into Muslim Bengal, seeking protection under the British Raj. The Burmese also took many prisoners from the region, whom they relocated to central Burma, leaving Arakan sparsely populated. Almost a century later, in 1885, the British (over the course of three Anglo-Burmese wars) had annexed the entire country of Burma and incorporated it into British India. They then encouraged labor migrants to move to Arakan for seasonal agricultural work, resulting in an increase in the population from neighboring Bengal territory. This colonial labor migration policy would later be used to justify claims that Rohingya were merely recent immigrants rather than indigenous inhabitants. During World War II, tensions escalated into communal violence, especially between pro-Japanese Arakanese and Muslim Arakanese fighting for the British. This bifurcated Arakan along ethno-religious lines. In the war's aftermath, Muslims who had fought for the British Empire argued for a Muslim state or the annexation into East Pakistan (Bangladesh today). Neither was granted, and Muslims who now dominated the northern region of Arakan were incorporated into the newly independent Burma. It was during the post-independence period that Muslims in the region began to use the term "Rohingya" as a self-describing ethnonym in their political endeavors. This was a political necessity as the Muslim population of Burma was and is very diverse, and the struggles for self-determination in Arakan were not shared across the Muslim community. Thus, Rohingya became the ethnic identity ascribed to the Muslims of Arakan to differentiate their quest for national belonging and inclusion.

However, the Rohingya's claims to belonging in Myanmar have been systematically contested by the Myanmar state. The 1982 Burma Citizenship

Law explicitly excluded Rohingya from the list of recognized ethnic groups, rendering them stateless by declaring them as "non-national" or "foreign residents" (Refugees International 2009, 36; Human Rights Watch 2000). The military regime used arbitrary and discriminatory means that spanned the legal, political, and economic domains to limit Rohingya participation in politics, education, economic, social, and civic life. This led to many Rohingya becoming effectively stateless in their own country. Ongoing political tensions escalated over the twentieth century with several mass expulsions of Rohingya across the border to Bangladesh. This legal exclusion has escalated into what international observers, including UN investigators, have termed genocide, with scholars similarly characterizing the Rohingya's systematic persecution as genocide (Green et al. 2015). In late 2012, large-scale mob violence encouraged by the Bamar-dominated Buddhist government saw scores of Rohingya killed or displaced; many survivors were forced into internment camps (Physicians for Human Rights 2013). The Myanmar military's systematic campaigns of violence against Rohingya civilians, including mass killings, rape, and the burning of entire villages, represent what scholars have called a "slow-burning genocide" that has intensified dramatically since 2012 (Zarni and Cowley 2014). As a result of this persecution, hundreds of thousands have fled their homes to neighboring Bangladesh, and onward to predominantly Malaysia, where a sizable diaspora has been established. The experience of systematic persecution and statelessness profoundly shapes how Rohingya refugees experience life in Malaysia (O'Brien and Hoffstaedter 2020), influencing everything from their encounters with Malaysian authorities (chapters 3 and 5) to their strategies for maintaining cultural identity (chapter 7).

The different historical trajectories of Chin and Rohingya displacement have resulted in starkly different treatment by both the UNHCR and the Malaysian government. These differences expose how religion, geopolitics, and international advocacy networks shape refugee protection in practice. Chin refugees have benefited from advocacy from Christian organizations in resettlement countries, particularly the United States, where evangelical groups have lobbied for their protection. Since the early 2000s, the UNHCR has resettled Chin refugees in large numbers to the United States and Australia, creating substantial transnational diaspora communities that provide both financial and political support for those remaining in Malaysia. However, this resettlement pathway has also meant that Chin refugees have never been encouraged to integrate into Malaysian society. The assumption has always been that Malaysia represents a temporary transit point before resettlement elsewhere. In 2015, as the security situation in Myanmar appeared to improve, the UNHCR even encouraged Chin refugees to return to Myanmar voluntarily, a policy that proved premature given the subsequent military coup in 2021. It was subsequently quietly reversed by the UNHCR.

Rohingya refugees, by contrast, have experienced a more complex relationship with Malaysian protection. Malaysia's identity as a Muslim-majority country has created expectations among Rohingya that they would receive sanctuary based on religious solidarity. Some early-arriving Rohingya refugees in the 1970s and 1980s did achieve a degree of integration into Malaysian society, with some obtaining permanent residency and even citizenship. However, more recent Rohingya arrivals have faced increasing restrictions and hostility. The Malaysian government has been reluctant to provide formal protection to Rohingya refugees, partly due to concerns about encouraging further arrivals and partly due to diplomatic considerations with Myanmar. The UNHCR has not pursued large-scale resettlement for Rohingya refugees, instead focusing on local integration possibilities that have largely failed to materialize. Both refugee populations in Malaysia exhibit distinct demographic patterns that reflect the gendered nature of displacement and labor migration. Approximately two-thirds of both Chin and Rohingya refugees are men, with one-third women. This gender imbalance reflects the fact that men are often the first to migrate, seeking work opportunities that will allow them to support families who remain in Myanmar or have fled to other countries. Both refugee populations also display significant diversity in terms of educational background, class position, and family circumstances, all factors that profoundly affect their mobility options and survival strategies in Malaysia.

MALAYSIA AS CRUCIAL PROTECTION SPACE

Malaysia occupies a unique and contradictory position in Southeast Asia's refugee landscape. The region hosts almost three million people of concern according to UNHCR figures, yet refugee policy across Southeast Asia has been driven primarily by states' efforts to counter human trafficking and increase border protection rather than enhance protection for displaced populations. This represents a "protection deficit," i.e., a systematic failure to develop adequate legal and institutional frameworks for refugee rights. The legal vacuum is striking: among the Association of Southeast Asian Nations (ASEAN) eleven member states, only three (Timor-Leste, the Philippines, and Cambodia) are signatories to the 1951 UN Refugee Convention and its 1967 Protocol. Malaysia, despite hosting one of the region's largest refugee populations, has consistently refused to sign these legal protection instruments. Its non-signatory status reflects a deliberate policy choice that allows the Malaysian state to maintain flexibility in how it treats refugees while avoiding international legal obligations (Hoffstaedter and Jalil 2025).

Malaysia's emergence as a crucial protection space is paradoxical. The country has gained a reputation as a refugee transit hub, particularly for Christian ethnic minorities from Myanmar who could expect resettlement to the United States or Australia within a few years. This informal resettlement pathway made Malaysia attractive to refugees compared to neighboring Thailand, where Myanmar refugees are largely confined to camps, or India, where registration is slower and resettlement opportunities are minimal. Yet this protection is entirely contingent and revocable. Malaysia's Immigration Act makes refugees' presence illegal, placing them in the same legal category as undocumented economic migrants. According to current UNHCR figures, there are approximately 200,000 registered refugees and asylum seekers in West Malaysia as of 2025, with the vast majority — nearly 180,000 — originating from Myanmar (UNHCR Malaysia 2025). The Myanmar refugee population comprises 117,670 Rohingya, 29,620 Chin, and 31,730 individuals from other ethnic groups fleeing conflict-affected areas or persecution. Beyond Myanmar nationals, Malaysia hosts approximately 21,230 refugees and asylum seekers from 50 other countries, including significant populations from Pakistan (5,650), Yemen (3,050), Somalia (2,780), Afghanistan (2,770), Syria (2,520), Sri Lanka (1,030), Palestine (500), Iraq (440), and other nations affected by war and persecution. The demographic composition shows that 64 percent of refugees and asylum seekers are men, while 36 percent are women, with children under 18 comprising 59,250 individuals, which is nearly 30 percent of the total population (UNHCR Malaysia 2025).

Refugees in Malaysia thus inhabit a legal limbo that creates a "precarious protection," i.e., a form of sanctuary that exists despite, rather than because of, state policy. Refugees like Rahman can access work in the informal economy and avoid the physical confinement of refugee camps, but they remain vulnerable to arbitrary detention, deportation, and exploitation. Their "protection" depends entirely on the discretion of individual employers, landlords, and officials rather than on any systematic guarantee of rights. Malaysia's approach to refugee protection operates through what can be described as "strategic ambiguity," or the deliberate policy of neither fully recognizing nor completely rejecting the presence of refugees. This ambiguity serves multiple functions: it allows Malaysia to benefit from cheap refugee labor while avoiding the costs of formal integration; it provides flexibility to respond to changing regional dynamics; and it deflects international pressure by pointing to the presence of the UNHCR while maintaining that refugee protection is not Malaysia's responsibility (Jalil and Hoffstaedter 2024).

FIGURE 1 Market and apartment buildings with high refugee concentration close to the city center of Kuala Lumpur

The Malaysian government has, at different times, provided temporary protection arrangements for specific groups. Acehnese refugees received IMM13 visas, which allowed them to work and live legally post-tsunami, during the early 2000s, and there have been periodic discussions about providing work permits for Rohingya refugees (Hoffstaedter 2015). However, these arrangements are always temporary, revocable, and dependent on broader political considerations rather than principled commitments to refugee rights. This informal system of accommodation means that refugees' experiences vary dramatically depending on their ethnicity, religion, time of arrival, and individual circumstances. Some early-arriving Rohingya refugees achieved a degree of integration into Malaysian society, while more recent arrivals face greater restrictions and hostility.

The contradiction at the heart of Malaysia's refugee policy is that economic integration proceeds alongside systematic social and political exclusion. Refugees are essential to Malaysia's economy, working in what are called "3D" jobs: dirty, dangerous, and demeaning work that Malaysian citizens increasingly reject. Refugees staff restaurant kitchens, work on palm oil plantations, labor on construction sites, and, like Rahman, perform essential services in wet markets and other informal sectors. This economic dependence creates a peculiar form of conditional hospitality. Refugees are tolerated, even welcomed, as workers, but they remain unwelcome as people with rights, needs, and aspirations beyond their labor power. The COVID-19 pandemic starkly revealed this contradiction: refugees who had been economically essential suddenly became medically threatening, illustrating how quickly conditional acceptance can transform into active hostility. Malaysia's position as a crucial protection space in Southeast Asia thus represents not a model of humanitarian leadership but rather a case study in how states can benefit from refugee presence while avoiding responsibility for refugee protection. This systemic precarity has significant implications for how we understand both refugee agency and state sovereignty in the contemporary global order, themes I explore throughout the book, particularly in chapter 4's analysis of place-making under polycrisis conditions.

METHODOLOGY

This study[2] employed a multi-sited ethnographic fieldwork approach to understand the complex and varied experiences of refugees living in Malaysia. The research was predominately conducted over a 12-month period from 2015 to 2017, building upon ten years of prior ethnographic research experience in Malaysia and extensive networks within refugee communities established through pilot studies conducted between 2009 and 2012. The extended timeframe was essential for developing the deep, trust-based relationships fundamental to ethical ethnographic research with vulnerable populations, relationships that prove crucial for understanding the place-making strategies.

Drawing on anthropological traditions that employ reflexive methods (Harrell-Bond and Voutira 1992), this research positioned the researcher not as an advocate for so-called voiceless people, but as a cultural intermediary working to build bridges for better understanding and create interstitial spaces for intercultural engagement that allow different lifeworlds to

2 The research that underpins this project was supported by an Australian Research Council Discovery Early Career Researcher Award (DECRA) DE140100052. This methodology section draws on ethical clearance obtained from the University of Queensland Behavioural and Social Sciences Ethical Review Committee (BSSERC) (clearance no. 2015000349) and follows the National Statement on Ethical Conduct in Human Research guidelines for research with vulnerable populations.

become mutually intelligible through cultural translation (Hoffstaedter 2013; Sanford and Angel-Ajani 2006). This approach aligns with contemporary scholarship that emphasizes refugee agency and the politics of representation in forced migration research (Harrell-Bond and Voutira 1992; Malkki 1995b; Sigona 2014). This approach also challenges traditional humanitarian narratives that often construct refugees as passive victims, instead recognizing their active role in meaning-making and survival strategies (Harrell-Bond 1986). This process relied fundamentally on immersion with a range of refugees, organizations, and groups, and the kindness and support of the people with whom I worked.

Fieldwork was primarily conducted in the Klang Valley urban conglomeration, stretching from Kuala Lumpur to the port of Klang, where most refugees in West Malaysia reside, to access established refugee communities, employment opportunities in the large informal sector, and UNHCR registration services. Additional fieldwork was conducted in regional centers, including Penang, the Cameron Highlands, Batu Arang, and remote plantation areas, to capture the diversity of refugee settlement patterns across peninsular Malaysia. Extensive participant observation formed the cornerstone of the research methodology, involving sustained engagement with refugee communities over the full year of fieldwork. This approach follows established anthropological methods for conducting research with marginalized populations, emphasizing the importance of long-term relationship building and trust development (Jackson 2002; Turner 2016). The methodology draws on scholarship highlighting the significance of ethnographic immersion for understanding the everyday experiences of urban refugees and the ways they navigate exclusion and create belonging (Grabska 2006; Jansen 2008). This included living with refugees, participating in their daily activities, attending community events, religious gatherings, and informal social interactions. The prolonged nature of this engagement was crucial for understanding the nuanced ways refugees navigate their daily lives, create social networks, and develop strategies for survival and belonging in Malaysia's challenging legal environment.

The research involved conducting over 80 formal interviews with refugees over the 12-month period, complemented by countless informal conversations that emerged through participant observation. Interview participants were drawn primarily from Rohingya and Chin communities, representing the largest refugee populations in Malaysia, as well as smaller numbers from other Myanmar ethnic groups, including Myanmar Muslims, Karen, Karenni, and Kachin refugees. Interviews employed both structured and unstructured formats, depending on the context and participant preferences.

Many interviews were conducted as life history narratives, allowing participants to share their experiences in their own words and according to their own priorities. This approach proved particularly important given the traumatic nature of many participants' experiences and the need to center their agency in the research process.

FIGURE 2 Building rapport through shared activities, such as a fishing trip with Chin refugee community members

Recognition of cultural sensitivities around gender interactions was central to the interview methodology. My wife, who is a trained oral historian, played an instrumental role in facilitating interviews with Rohingya and Chin women, enabling access to perspectives and experiences that would otherwise have been difficult to capture (e.g., see Lamb and Hoffstaedter 2020). This collaborative approach was essential for understanding the gendered dimensions of refugee experiences, including challenges and survival strategies specific to women. The presence of my partner also enabled more nuanced data collection about family dynamics, child-rearing practices, and women's community networks. Many female participants expressed greater comfort discussing sensitive topics related to displacement trauma, family separation, and experiences of discrimination when speaking with another woman, especially in the Rohingya community.

Additionally, I recruited a team of research assistants from host and relevant refugee communities, including individuals with Myanmar Muslim, Rohingya, Chin, Burmese, and Malay backgrounds. This community-based approach was essential for several reasons: it provided cultural brokerage and translation services, facilitated access to community networks, and helped address the inherent power imbalances between researcher and participants (Fiddian-Qasmiyeh et al. 2014). The approach aligns with scholarship that emphasizes the importance of community participation in refugee research and the value of insider knowledge for understanding marginalized experiences (Kaiser 2005; Jacobsen 2005). Comprehensive training was provided to research assistants in ethical research conduct, interview techniques, and documenting oral testimonies. This training covered informed consent procedures, confidentiality protocols, trauma-informed interviewing approaches, and methods for supporting participants who became distressed during interviews. The training also emphasized the importance of community ownership of the research process and ways to ensure that participation benefited community members. Research assistants often worked independently within their communities, conducting interviews and facilitating connections with potential participants. This approach was particularly important given the precarious legal status of refugees and the need to avoid exposing participants to additional risks through research participation.

FIGURE 3 Interviewing Rohingya grass-cutters in their container home/ workplace

Beyond refugee community members, the research included interviews with key stakeholders representing different aspects of Malaysia's refugee landscape. This encompassed Malaysian civil society representatives, including staff from local non-governmental organizations (NGOs), community organizations, and advocacy groups working with refugees; community leaders and representatives, both formal and informal leaders within refugee communities who play key roles in community organizing and advocacy; international organization staff, including UNHCR representatives and staff from international NGOs providing services to refugees; Malaysian society members, including employers who hire refugees, landlords, neighbors, and others who interact with refugees in daily life; and expatriate supporters, long-term expatriate residents involved in refugee support activities and community work. These stakeholder interviews provided crucial context for understanding the broader social, political, and economic environment within which refugees navigate their lives in Malaysia, insights that prove particularly important for understanding the conditional nature of hospitality examined in chapter 2 and the strategic visibility employed in sporting activities analyzed in chapter 7.

Given the vulnerable legal status of refugees in Malaysia, extensive ethical safeguards were implemented throughout the research process. All names and identifying details have been changed to protect participant privacy and security. Data was stored on password-protected devices and in locked cabinets, with particular attention to ensure that participant information could not be accessed by authorities. This approach reflects scholarship on the ethical complexities of conducting research with undocumented populations and the need for enhanced confidentiality measures (Good 2007; Kibreab 2004). The research approach prioritized beneficence, following the National Statement on Ethical Conduct in Human Research principle that research should provide meaningful benefit to participants and communities. As an engaged anthropologist, my research always aims to bear witness to refugee experiences and document stories that might otherwise remain unheard, while being mindful of the potential consequences of academic work for the communities being studied. Research assistants were provided with information about local support services and community resources to connect participants with assistance if needed. The embedded nature of research assistants within their own communities meant they could provide ongoing support and follow-up contact with participants beyond the formal research interaction.

Data collection involved multiple methods, including audio recording of interviews (with consent), detailed field notes from participant observation, photography of community events and activities, and collection of relevant documents such as community newsletters and policy materials. The multi-method approach provided both breadth and depth, enabling analysis of individual experiences alongside broader patterns of exclusion and belonging, an analysis that forms the foundation for the comparative examination of Chin and Rohingya experiences throughout the book. Field notes were maintained daily and included both observational data and reflexive commentary on the research process, researcher positionality, and emerging analytical insights. Regular debriefing sessions were held with research assistants to ensure ethical standards were maintained and to incorporate their insights into the ongoing research process. The ethnographic data were analyzed through a reflexive, iterative process that sought to center refugee voices while providing rigorous scholarly analysis. This involved ongoing reflection on questions of representation, reciprocity, and the potential consequences of academic work for research participants and their communities. Analysis focused on understanding both individual experiences and broader structural patterns, examining how refugees create meaning, build social connections, and develop strategies for navigating Malaysia's complex social and legal environment. The longitudinal nature of the fieldwork enabled analysis of how experiences and strategies changed over time in response to shifting circumstances and policy changes.

THEORETICAL CONTRIBUTIONS

This book makes several interconnected theoretical contributions that build upon and extend existing scholarship in refugee studies, urban anthropology, and Southeast Asian studies. The concept of "radical othering" (Hoffstaedter 2011b) provides a framework for understanding how refugees are positioned within host societies that goes beyond traditional concepts of difference developed in postcolonial theory. While scholars like Edward Said and Homi Bhabha focused primarily on colonial relationships and cultural difference, the refugee experience in Malaysia reveals forms of exclusion that operate through different mechanisms and serve different functions. Radical othering, as I conceptualize it throughout this book but particularly in the analysis of daily urban encounters and the examination of conditional hospitality, refers to the systematic process by which refugees are positioned as fundamentally outside the normal categories of social and political belonging. Unlike other forms of othering that still acknowledge the "other" as part of a shared social universe, radical othering places refugees in what Giorgio Agamben (1998) calls a "state of exception," i.e., a space where normal rules and categories cease to apply.

In Malaysia's context, this process is particularly complex because it operates within an already intricate system of ethnic categorization. Malaysia's official multiculturalism recognizes three main ethnic groups: Malay or *bumiputera* (sons of the soil), Chinese, and Indian. Refugees, however, exist outside the state-maintained categories; neither incorporated into an existing ethnic category nor acknowledged as a separate category deserving recognition. This positioning serves multiple functions: it creates a scapegoat for societal tensions (Girard 1986), deflects attention from Malaysia's deep-seated racial and political divisions, and reinforces Malaysian national identity through contrast with the excluded "them" (Hoffstaedter 2017b). Malaysia's multicultural yet ethnically divided society tolerates refugees through informal mechanisms like UNHCR operations while simultaneously denying them formal legal recognition, creating what I describe as a liminal, extra-legal "non-place" that reinforces their marginalization (Van Houtum and Van Naerssen 2002). As the "radical other," refugees stand outside Malaysia's ethnicized political discourse and daily confrontations, making them vulnerable to discrimination without repercussions to the wider body politic. The concept is particularly evident in the treatment of minorities within minority groups like Chin refugees, who represent multiple layers of otherness: Christian in a Muslim-majority state, racially resembling Chinese, another Malaysian minority, and residing as undocumented immigrants.

This radical otherness has paradoxical effects. On the one hand, it renders refugees invisible to official policy and excludes them from normal political processes, leaving them trapped in the "politics of (in)visibility" (Hoffstaedter 2011b). On the other hand, as Jean Baudrillard (1993, 137–38) suggests, radical otherness can possess a "lingering presence" that destabilizes systems of domination. Refugees' very existence outside Malaysia's ethnic framework reveals the contingent and constructed nature of these categories, potentially opening spaces for alternative forms of political belonging. In previous work (Hoffstaedter 2014a, Hoffstaedter 2016), I demonstrate how this systematic exclusion serves broader political purposes while keeping refugees in a state of perpetual precariousness, unable to fully integrate into Malaysian society despite their physical presence within its borders.

Another important concept is that of place-making, as developed in human geography and urban studies. It typically refers to community-driven efforts to create meaningful, functional spaces that reflect local needs and identities. However, the refugee experience in Malaysia requires us to extend this concept to situations where place-making occurs within fundamentally hostile environments characterized by legal exclusion, economic exploitation, and social marginalization. Refugee place-making in Malaysia operates through "sociabilities of emplacement" (Çağlar and Glick Schiller 2018), i.e., the informal networks, practices, and spaces through which refugees create forms of belonging despite their systematic exclusion. These sociabilities include: transforming apartment buildings into informal community centers; creating parallel educational systems for refugee children; developing rotating credit associations that provide financial security; and establishing religious and cultural spaces that maintain connections to the homeland while adapting to Malaysian contexts. Crucially, these place-making activities are not simply adaptive responses to exclusion but represent forms of agency that can unsettle dominant ideas about Malaysian national identity. When refugees create communities, establish successful businesses, or develop innovative survival strategies, they challenge narratives about Malaysian society that depend on their exclusion and marginalization. However, refugee place-making also operates within severe constraints.

The constant threat of immigration raids, detention, and deportation means that refugees must develop forms of belonging that remain invisible to state authorities. Their place-making strategies thus involve a delicate balance between creating meaningful community life and maintaining the low profile necessary for survival.

One theoretical challenge in refugee studies is how to acknowledge refugee agency without minimizing the structural constraints that shape their lives. The experiences of Chin and Rohingya refugees in Malaysia reveal forms of agency that operate within, rather than against, systems of exclusion and exploitation. This constrained agency manifests in several ways: the strategic use of religious and ethnic identities to access protection networks; the development of informal labor arrangements that provide economic security while remaining technically illegal; the creation of transnational connections that allow refugees to maintain homeland ties while building new lives in Malaysia; and the tactical deployment of "refugeeness" as a form of social capital that can sometimes elicit sympathy or assistance. These forms of agency are not heroic resistance against oppression but rather practical strategies people develop to survive and thrive in impossible circumstances. Thus, they represent what James Scott (1985) calls "weapons of the weak," forms of everyday resistance that work within systems of power rather than directly challenging them.

This book makes several specific contributions to understanding migration and displacement in Southeast Asia. First, it centers the experiences of transit countries rather than focusing primarily on the source or destination countries of refugees. This shift in perspective reveals how transit countries like Malaysia are not merely passive way stations but active participants in shaping refugee experiences through their policies of strategic ambiguity. Second, the book contributes to debates about ASEAN's approach to human rights and refugee protection. Rather than simply critiquing ASEAN's limitations, I argue that the organization's principle of non-interference actually enables a form of regional governance that benefits from refugee labor while avoiding responsibility for refugee protection. This represents a particular form of "organized irresponsibility" that requires new analytical frameworks. Third, the book extends critical multiculturalism debates to the refugee context. Malaysia's official multiculturalism has been extensively analyzed by scholars, but the position of refugees outside this multicultural (or multiracial) system reveals important dynamics about how multicultural frameworks can simultaneously include and exclude different populations.

Furthermore, the book's focus on two specific ethnic groups allows for comparative analysis that contrasts both similarities and differences in refugee experiences. This comparative approach allows us to see how factors such as religion, education, international advocacy networks, and host-country policies interact to shape protection outcomes in complex ways. The following chapter provides a detailed account of the history of both Rohingya and Chin, as well as their migration patterns to Malaysia.

CHAPTER 1

Historical Trajectories and Contemporary Patterns of Chin and Rohingya Migration to Malaysia

Malaysia has emerged as a crucial protection space for refugees in Southeast Asia, hosting approximately 200,000 refugees and asylum seekers from Myanmar (UNHCR 2025), though the actual figure is likely double that. Among these displaced populations, two groups predominate: the Rohingya, a Muslim minority from Rakhine State, and the Chin, a largely Christian ethnic minority from Myanmar's mountainous northwest. Together, these communities represent the largest contingent of refugees in Malaysia, yet their paths to displacement, migration routes, and settlement experiences differ markedly due to distinct historical trajectories, religious identities, and relationships with both the Myanmar state and Malaysian society. Understanding how these groups came to Malaysia in large numbers requires examining not only contemporary persecution in Myanmar but also the deeper historical forces that shaped ethnic boundaries, the different migration networks they utilized, and the complex organizational structures they developed. This chapter shows how historical administrative practices continue to influence displacement patterns, how religious identity shapes reception in Malaysia, and how refugee communities have developed sophisticated systems to navigate their precarious legal status.

ROHINGYA: FROM ARAKAN KINGDOM TO SYSTEMATIC PERSECUTION

The Rohingya can trace their presence in the historical Arakan region of modern-day Myanmar to significant historical depth, with connections to the medieval Arakan kingdom of Mrauk U, which flourished between the fifteenth and eighteenth centuries. This kingdom maintained strong connections with Islamic sultanates in the Indian subcontinent, particularly Bengal, and engaged in centuries of cultural and religious exchange. Muslim merchants, scholars, and settlers had established communities along the coast since at least the eighth century, creating a foundational Islamic presence that predated later colonial interventions. During the Arakan kingdom period, the porous borders between Bengal and Arakan allowed for continued movement and settlement of Muslim populations in this strategically important coastal region. However, British colonial administrative practices created lasting divisions through tools such as the census, which helped codify identities that were once more malleable, flexible, and open to newcomers (Furnivall 1948). The late eighteenth-century Burmese conquest of Arakan in 1784 triggered the first major wave of Muslim displacement, with many fleeing to British Bengal for protection. When the British later annexed Burma in 1885 and incorporated it into British India, they encouraged labor migration from Bengal to work in Arakan's agricultural sector, significantly increasing the Muslim population. This colonial-era migration intensified ethnic and religious tensions, particularly during World War II, when communal violence erupted between pro-Japanese Buddhist Arakanese and Muslim Arakanese fighting alongside the British forces. Following Burma's independence, the Muslim population's failed attempts to join East Pakistan led to decades of systematic discrimination by successive military governments. The newly adopted "Rohingya" ethnic identity emerged during the 1950s–60s as Muslims in Arakan sought political recognition and self-determination. However, this period marked the beginning of severe restrictions on Rohingya participation in political, educational, and economic life, effectively rendering hundreds of thousands stateless and triggering multiple mass expulsions to Bangladesh throughout the twentieth century.

The ongoing persecution has created a vast Rohingya diaspora, with hundreds of thousands fleeing to neighboring Bangladesh and establishing refugee camps there. Beyond Bangladesh, large communities have formed in Malaysia, Saudi Arabia, and Pakistan, where Rohingya often live as undocumented workers or temporary labor migrants without legal status. Malaysia has become a significant destination due to its proximity and existing Muslim communities, though most Rohingya there face precarious circumstances without official recognition or protection, adding further hardship to their displacement experience, as I will elaborate on in subsequent chapters below. The Rohingya case exemplifies how the transformation of ethnic identities under colonialism and the movement of peoples and borders have lasting effects. While the historical evidence shows that Rohingya can trace their historical roots in the region to the Arakan kingdom, a Buddhist kingdom heavily influenced by neighboring Islamic sultanates, this heritage is continually questioned and denied in modern Myanmar. It is important to remember how porous and malleable borders have historically been, and how easily they have been traversed and settled by various peoples. The closing of borders, their securitization, and the expulsion of people no longer deemed part of the body politic are profoundly modern phenomena.

CHIN: MISSIONARY INFLUENCE AND LINGUISTIC FRAGMENTATION

The Chin experience, meanwhile, reflects the complex interaction between pre-colonial ethnic identity, colonial administrative systems, and missionary linguistic policies. While the name "Chin" has ancient origins reaching back around 1,000 years and was used "from the very beginning not only by the Chin themselves but also by neighboring peoples, such as the Kachin, Shan and Burman" (Sakhong 2003, 3), British colonial authorities fundamentally reshaped how this identity was administratively organized and linguistically standardized. The British established administrative systems that consolidated what the Chin scholar Sakhong (2003, 17) identifies as "six major tribal groups of the Chin, namely the 1) Asho, 2) Chó or Sho, 3) Khuami or M'ro, 4) Laimi, 5) Mizo (Lushai) and 6) Zomi" under unified administrative structures. Historical evidence shows that "the Chin were known by no other name than CHIN until they made their settlement in 'Chin Nwe'" but subsequently "split into different tribal groups with different tribal names and dialects" after their dispersal from the Chindwin Valley (Sakhong 2003, 16–17). Much like across the British Empire, the Chin Hills were administered using both the classic divide-and-rule and the British classification system to split peoples into convenient ethnic and religious identities and make them legible to the colonial administrative system. The British implemented the Circle Administration system, which divided the Chin Hills into bounded and defined territories and diminished existing indigenous systems of governance. Alongside the governmental reordering, the British amalgamated several local groups into a unified Chin identity with a singular legal system (Sakhong 2003, 102). After political unification, the British attempted to enforce linguistic unification by making the Laizo dialect the sole language for all education.

The arrival of American missionaries in the late nineteenth century created a new unifying force among these diverse communities. Christian conversion became widespread, transforming formerly animist tribes and creating the foundation for a modern Chin identity centered around evangelical Christianity. This religious transformation became both a source of unity and a target for later persecution by Myanmar's Buddhist-majority state, dynamics that are crucial for understanding how Chin refugees navigate religious networks in Malaysia. However, missionary politics also intervened to maintain linguistic difference, for example, under Rev. J. H. Cope, who became influential in local policymaking on education for both the Christian mission and the colonial power. He "insisted on the use of three dialects, or what came to be known as the three standard dialects: Kamhau dialect, Lai (Haka) dialect and Laizo (Falam) dialect" (Sakhong 2003, 167). Debates continue over whether a single lingua franca or a common dialect would have been (and may still be) a key unifying element in the political struggle, or whether diversity must persist to strengthen regional and local identities.

The colonial period created divergent experiences among Chin tribal groups. Notably, "the Zomi from the Tiddim and Tawnzang areas followed the orders of the British colonial power and sent men to France during World War I" as a labor corps, while groups like the Laimi "fought the war at home" during the Anglo-Chin War of 1917–19 (Sakhong 2003, 160–61). These different experiences contributed to distinct postwar trajectories and have influenced contemporary debates about identity and nomenclature, particularly regarding claims about "Zo" versus "Chin" identity. Today, "Chin" functions as both a state-designated ethnic category with deep historical roots and an administrative term that encompasses significant internal diversity. The tension between this overarching identity and sub-group identities continues to manifest in contemporary debates about nomenclature and representation, complicated by the colonial legacy of both administrative consolidation and linguistic fragmentation that has persisted into the post-independence period.

The British Empire's approach to managing plural societies has left lasting impacts across Southeast Asia and beyond. Plural societies, such as Malaysia and Myanmar, had their populace systematically categorized so the British colonial power could better control and rule them (Furnivall 1948). The colonial census emerged as a particularly powerful tool, with lasting consequences: identities that were once malleable and relatively open became closed, and their boundaries were policed. The Myanmar government continues to use these imperial tools of divide and conquer to classify and control its population, albeit with diminishing success after the 2021 coup.

CONTEMPORARY DISPLACEMENT DYNAMICS AND SETTLEMENT PRACTICES

Contemporary persecution and displacement patterns reflect these deep historical roots while taking on new dimensions of violence and exclusion culminating in what scholars term systematic persecution amounting to genocide (Green et al. 2015). Legal exclusion began with the 1982 Citizenship Law, which effectively rendered them stateless by classifying them as foreign residents rather than citizens (Human Rights Watch 2000). This legal framework was built upon colonial-era arguments about Bengali immigration to justify contemporary exclusion. Recent violence has dramatically intensified displacement pressures. The 2012 communal clashes in Rakhine State resulted in thousands of deaths and widespread displacement, predominantly affecting Rohingya communities (Physicians for Human Rights 2013). These conflicts created lasting trauma that extends beyond Myanmar's borders, affecting refugee communities even in places of supposed safety.

The systematic nature of persecution encompasses multiple dimensions: legal exclusion, economic marginalization, restrictions on movement and education, and periodic outbreaks of severe violence (Fortify Rights 2014). This multifaceted oppression has created sustained displacement pressures affecting multiple generations of Rohingya families. Chin displacement primarily stems from religious persecution and military oppression targeting Christian minorities. Myanmar's military has systematically attacked Christian symbols and religious leaders, with many refugees reporting specific incidents involving the destruction of crosses and persecution of pastors (Chin Human Rights Organization 2012a). This religious targeting reflects broader policies of forced assimilation that seek to homogenize Myanmar's diverse population under Buddhist-Bamar dominance. Military oppression takes multiple forms, including forced labor and conscription into porter service; the latter involves compelling civilians to carry heavy supplies across mountainous terrain under harsh conditions, often accompanied by physical abuse and inadequate provisions (Shan Human Rights Foundation 2002). Many who have fled Myanmar to Malaysia describe escaping during these forced labor assignments.

Active conflict between ethnic armies and Myanmar's military has created additional displacement pressures. Many stories of flight from Chin State describe how ordinary villagers became caught in the crossfire between the Chin National Army and government forces. For example, Van and Ruth, a couple I stayed with for several weeks, described how, in the early 2000s, fighting in their area led to the widespread conscription of local men for porter duties, forcing them to eventually flee to Thailand and later Malaysia.

At the time, they were living in a small hamlet not far from Hakha, the capital of Chin State. Their lives were increasingly shaped by the intensifying conflict between the Chin National Army and the Myanmar military. The Chin Hills were and remain contested territory. The Myanmar Army maintained an extensive military presence there, with bases occupying strategic mountain ridges from which they conducted extensive patrols. The Chin National Front (CNF) operated in the same areas, establishing bases near civilian villages. Van and Ruth's community found itself in trouble as both armed groups demanded money, food, and labor from the villagers.

The Myanmar Army commandeered local men for portering duties, forcing them to carry heavy military supplies and 25-kilogram bags of rice through steep mountainous terrain. Porters faced beatings and were given substandard and insufficient food. Thus, many who survived these assignments fled at the first opportunity rather than face re-conscription. When fighting escalated in their area and men from a nearby village were conscripted for porter duty, the couple decided to run, not wanting Van to be next. With only hours to prepare, they packed essentials and left their village, heading first to the central city of Mandalay and then onwards to Yangon. There, a contact from a childhood friend connected them with a smuggling agent. They did not trust the first agent and settled on an agent who had successfully brought a family member to Malaysia. Their journey involved multiple stages: a van journey through southeastern Myanmar, a difficult jungle trek across the Myanmar-Thai border with about 20 people guided by two smugglers, another van journey through Thailand, a second arduous trek across the Thai-Malaysian border, and finally transport by car to Kuala Lumpur.

Migration routes to Malaysia reflect both the constraints imposed by persecution and the opportunities created by existing networks and geographical proximity. Rohingya migration to Malaysia predominantly involves dangerous sea crossings across the Andaman Sea, often aboard overcrowded, unseaworthy vessels (Hoffstaedter and Missbach 2022). These journeys frequently begin as consensual smuggling arrangements but transform into trafficking situations as costs escalate and passengers become captive to extortion (Grundy-Warr and Wong 2002). Thus, the maritime routes involve multiple stages of vulnerability, from initial sea crossings to land-based trafficking camps in Thailand, before final passage to Malaysia. The transformation from voluntary migration to coercive trafficking reflects the predatory nature of smuggling networks that exploit refugee desperation (Hoffstaedter and Missbach 2021; Hoffstaedter 2023).

Aminah's journey illustrates the lived reality of this transformation from consensual smuggling to coercive trafficking, revealing the specific mechanisms through which vulnerable people become trapped in predatory systems.[1] Aminah was a young Rohingya mother with four children whom we interviewed shortly after she arrived in Malaysia. She told us her story of flight and the journey across the Andaman Sea so many Rohingya have taken before her and continue to embark on today. Aminah and her husband paid smugglers a significant sum they had earned "by working hard in Burma," hoping and believing it would secure passage to Malaysia, where her husband's relatives could provide further support. The boat journey was extremely arduous with all passengers, children and adults alike, receiving only small portions of rice twice daily, without curry or other sustenance. "We as parents kept our rice for our children to eat in the afternoon," Aminah explained through tears. "I felt very sad and hopeless when I couldn't give my children rice when they were hungry, but I am thankful to God for bringing us to Malaysia safely." This deliberate nutritional deprivation serves two purposes: reducing the smugglers' costs while softening passengers for subsequent extortion.

Upon reaching Thailand, the promised journey ended abruptly. Smugglers demanded additional payments far exceeding the terms of the initial agreement. When Aminah and her husband could not pay, the transformation from smuggling to trafficking became explicit. "We paid the smuggler … but when we reached Thailand, we couldn't pay the smuggler again when they asked for money. Therefore, we were detained for two months," she recounted. The physical violence accompanying this detention left visible marks: "I was pushed by the smuggler and got injured in my leg."

The smugglers often separate families, especially men from their wives and children. Torture and rape are common in such trafficking camps. When Aminah tried to protect her husband from beatings, she too was assaulted: "I left my children and ran to my husband because he was being beaten up by the smugglers. Finally, we were separated by beating both of us." Subsequently, they were forced to call their relatives in Malaysia to pay ran-

1 Aminah's story is based on August 2015 fieldwork interviews.

soms for their freedom. The two-month detention period involved constant negotiation and escalating demands. Aminah's neighbors and friends from her village who knew the smugglers eventually paid RM 1,000 (USD 250) to secure the release of Aminah and her children, but her husband remained captive because they "couldn't pay as much as they asked." The smugglers were themselves Rohingya, operating camps with Thai personnel who visited "four to five times" to oversee operations. This ethnic dimension complicated straightforward victim-perpetrator narratives as the trafficking network included Rohingya who had themselves once been refugees, now extracting profit from their community's desperate flight.

Aminah's eventual arrival in Malaysia came through relatives' ransom payments and the assistance of villagers connected to smuggling networks, but her husband remained in Thailand. She reached Selayang at night with four children, knowing no one, without documentation that would enable UNHCR access, and found refuge only through Komar Jahan's spontaneous compassion (see chapter 5). Her journey from paying customer to trafficking victim to dependent refugee reveals how the migration industry's predatory logic systematically transforms consensual arrangements into coerced servitude, targeting the most vulnerable while extracting maximum profit from extended family networks.

The ease with which Aminah's journey shifted from smuggling to trafficking reflects the structural features of regional migration networks. The initial payment secured transport to Thailand but included no guarantees beyond that point. Smugglers operated in stages, with each transition point enabling additional extortion. The camps straddling the Thai-Malaysian border functioned openly, suggesting official complicity (Hoffstaedter and Missbach 2021). Family networks extending to Malaysia became a liability rather than an asset, as smugglers leveraged these connections to extract more money from relatives who themselves lived precariously.

This case illustrates how individual refugee journeys embody broader patterns of exploitation within Southeast Asian migration systems. The smuggling-trafficking continuum operates not as clear categories but as fluid positions shaped by refugees' economic resources, social capital, and bargaining power. Those who pay substantial sums upfront may experience a relatively straightforward passage, while those who pay incrementally or rely on future payments face escalating vulnerability. Gender, age, and family composition further determine exposure to particular forms of violence and exploitation.

Chin migration patterns differ significantly from those of the Rohingya, typically involving overland routes and more systematic utilization of established networks. Many Chin refugees initially fled to India before learning about opportunities in Malaysia through diaspora connections. Information about employment prospects and resettlement possibilities spreads through community networks, enabling more informed decision-making about destination countries (McConnachie 2018). The typical journey involves multiple stages and countries. Many refugees travel overland from Myanmar to Thailand, then traverse the jungle border between Thailand and Malaysia with smuggler assistance. These journeys are often pre-arranged and prepaid from Myanmar, demonstrating more systematic organization compared to spontaneous maritime departures. Upon arrival in Malaysia, kinship and community networks immediately activate to provide initial accommodation and guidance through registration processes. These networks connect new arrivals with ethnic refugee organizations and facilitate integration into existing communities (Hoffstaedter 2015). Van and Ruth's experience shows the potency and role of extended networks in facilitating flight. Their journey involved "a series of friends, family, and agents to guide them across the borders to Thailand and, eventually, Malaysia." This demonstrates how remittances and transnational connections can enable systematic displacement rather than purely crisis-driven flight, networks that prove crucial for the place-making strategies I examine in later chapters.

Settlement patterns and community formation in Malaysia reflect both economic necessities and the varying tolerances of particular Malaysian communities for refugee presence. Both Rohingya and Chin communities have established significant concentrations in specific areas of the Klang Valley, Malaysia's primary urban region. These settlements reflect different adaptation strategies and relationships with Malaysian society. Selayang has emerged as a particularly important area for Rohingya settlement, centered around one of Kuala Lumpur's largest wet markets, where many find employment. The area has experienced demographic transformation, with Rohingya and Myanmar Muslim communities, including both refugees and migrant workers, establishing restaurants, shops, and service organizations (Azis 2014). This concentration provides both economic opportunities and community support, but also creates visibility that attracts government attention. The area's complex demographics create challenges for state surveillance, as authorities encounter mixed populations of documented workers, undocumented migrants, and refugees with varying legal statuses. This complexity provides some protection through anonymity, but also makes residents vulnerable to sweeping enforcement operations (Nah 2007).

FIGURE 4 Refugee-operated market stall in Selayang selling fresh produce

Beyond urban concentrations, some refugee communities have established agricultural settlements that offer different opportunities for community building and economic development. These farming endeavors, initially supported by UNHCR's Special Protection Fund, demonstrate innovative approaches to refugee livelihoods and place-making (Jacobsen 2005). The Batu Arang farming communities, established with assistance from the Catholic Church, bring together different ethnic groups, including Karen, Rakhine, and Chin refugees. These settlements provide opportunities for food production, community gathering, and relative safety from urban surveillance pressures. The agricultural model enables different forms of social organization and cultural maintenance compared to urban settlements (Brees 2010), dynamics I examine comprehensively in my analysis of farming as place-making in chapter 6.

COMMUNITY ORGANIZATIONS AND SUPPORT SYSTEMS

Malaysian refugee communities, particularly those from Myanmar, have developed sophisticated organizational structures that provide services often unavailable through official channels. These organizations operate along ethnic lines, reflecting homeland divisions while adapting to Malaysian circumstances (Hoffstaedter 2015). The Chin community has developed particularly elaborate organizational networks that reflect both unity and internal diversity. Multiple organizations serve different constituencies based on township origins, religious affiliations, and linguistic groups within the broader Chin category. Members can belong to several organizations simultaneously, accessing different services and maintaining various identity connections (Sakhong 2012). The umbrella organization Coalition of Burma Ethnics Malaysia (COBEM) demonstrates the sophistication of these networks, bringing together eight ethnic organizations representing different Myanmar minority groups. This coalition provides a unified voice for advocacy while enabling specialized services for different communities (Hoffstaedter 2015).

These organizations provide comprehensive services that often exceed those available through formal humanitarian systems, including employment placement, workplace advocacy, shelter assistance, education for children, and skills training for adults. Many organizations maintain direct relationships with employers, enabling rapid job placement for new arrivals (Hoffstaedter 2015). The financial structure of these organizations demonstrates community investment and self-reliance. Membership fees provide operational funding while connecting refugees to identification documents and protection networks. The average fee structure requires manageable contributions that provide immediate practical benefits. These organizations also demonstrate increasing sophistication and advocacy capacity, holding service providers accountable and demanding improved assistance.

Religious identity plays crucial roles in service provision and community organization, but also creates boundaries and tensions. For Rohingya communities, Islamic institutions provide important educational and social services, though these efforts often operate with limited resources and face various challenges. For example, in 2015, I visited a *madrasah* (religious school) in the Klang Valley run by a Rohingya *ustaz* (religious teacher). These madrasahs form the mainstay of Rohingya education. Here, students learn basic Islamic teachings, how to recite the Quran in Arabic, and some Malay language. Some basic numeracy is also taught alongside religious teachings. The ustaz mentioned that the biggest challenge is finding teachers, as most Rohingya themselves are poorly educated, a result of decades of the Myanmar government's policy to limit Rohingya access to education. Thus, there are few qualified teachers available to provide primary and secondary education.

The precarious nature of refugee support is highlighted by the fact that refugee causes usually cannot attract corporate giving or benefit from political point-scoring, meaning that many organizations and individuals who help refugees do so quietly and discreetly. Thus, it is not the sort of philanthropy that attracts people who want to bask in the social and political limelight. However, religious boundaries can create complications. One example involved tensions between Christian service providers and the Muslim community. In a small town in Johor state, members of a Christian church congregation became aware of Rohingya refugees living in their town and discovered that their children did not have access to any education. They decided to act as individuals coming together to address a need. They rented a small shop lot and began teaching English, Malay, and mathematics to some local Rohingya children. Within a couple of weeks, a local Malay ustaz approached them to ask why they were teaching Muslims. He feared that this was an attempt to convert the Rohingya to Christianity (Hoffstaedter 2017b).

Arguments ensued, but ultimately a compromise was reached: the children could continue their secular schooling (by Christian teachers) in the morning, but in the afternoon they had to go next door to attend Islamic classes and the weekly sermon at the mosque on Fridays. The ustaz managed to raise the required funds to set up a school of his own next door in a short period of time. This suggests that funding for Islamic causes is readily available and that, even without government support, individuals and Muslim organizations can still raise funds. The temporal patterns of support reflect broader Malaysian charitable practices: Much of the attention is seasonal, with Muslim Malaysians expressing the most support for and interest in refugees during Ramadan, especially at the Eid al-Fitr celebration at the end of the fasting month. As one NGO worker in Kuala Lumpur quipped, "At Ramadan, the poor and needy are fed, but the rest of the year no one cares."

UNHCR registration and recognition systems have evolved significantly in response to overwhelming caseloads and the need to manage diverse refugee populations effectively. The large-scale arrival of refugees in the early 2000s led UNHCR Malaysia to develop innovative registration approaches to manage caseloads on a tight budget. Mass registration drives, sometimes held in stadiums, attracted thousands of applicants from across the country and dramatically increased the number of registered refugees (Crisp, Obi, and Umlas 2012). These mass registration events created their own challenges, including unexpected ethnic compositions. Registration drives designed for specific groups often attracted others, leading to logistical complications and resource strains. The scale of movement generated by registration rumors demonstrated both refugee information networks and the desperation for official recognition (Wake and Yu 2018). Between 2008 and 2010, these approaches enabled the registration of 75,000 refugees, fundamentally changing the scale of officially recognized refugee populations in Malaysia. This rapid increase created policy tensions with Malaysian authorities while providing protection benefits for refugee communities (Crisp et al. 2012).

The registration process reveals ongoing complexities around ethnic identity and persecution documentation. Recognition systems emphasize ethnic identity verification rather than individual persecution circumstances, creating particular challenges for communities with fluid or contested identities (Kneebone 2010). Most Chin and Rohingya refugees lack written documentation, making oral testimony the primary means of establishing identity and persecution claims. However, lengthy displacement journeys and extended periods in transit countries can make memories of initial displacement difficult to verify according to formal standards (Goodwin-Gill and McAdam 2007). The emphasis on ethnic legibility reflects administrative convenience but can exclude individuals whose identities do not fit established categories or who lack community connections to verify their claims. This system reproduces some aspects of historical administrative categorization while adapting to contemporary refugee protection needs (Rajaram and Grundy-Warr 2007).

Contemporary challenges and future prospects for both refugee communities reflect the intersection of Malaysian domestic politics, regional diplomatic considerations, and international resettlement policies. The two communities experience significantly different treatment within Malaysian society and international resettlement systems. Over the years, Christian Chin and others were consistently prioritized for resettlement outside Malaysia, with Rohingya allegedly slated for integration in Malaysia. However, "the [Malaysian] government, with its specific interest in the biopolitical improvement of the Malays, has little political goodwill to include the dark-skinned, Bangladeshi-looking Muslim Rohingya as citizen subjects" (Azis 2014, 852). This differential treatment reflects complex factors, including religious considerations and racial perceptions.

The experience of Rohingya in Malaysia remains paradoxical: "Despite their prolonged refugee situation in Malaysia, the Rohingya are still often considered to be short-term stayers" (Azis 2014: 840). However, Rohingya favor Malaysia as a destination, not only for its relative prosperity, but also because of its Muslim identity (Hoffstaedter 2017b). Education emerges as a crucial factor affecting community prospects and individual mobility. In Azis' fieldwork in the Klang Valley, literacy became a key issue of differentiation; without it, Rohingya were delegated to menial tasks and even likened to animals, as by one Malaysian respondent, who told her that "as long as [Rohingya] remain illiterate, the Rohingya animals will continue to be preyed upon by lurking predators" (Azis 2014, 847). The prolonged discrimination against Rohingya in Myanmar has meant that few refugees are educated or even literate, limiting their ability to work in anything beyond manual labor jobs, which also highlights the importance of education for survival and acceptance (Preston 1991).

INTERCOMMUNITY RELATIONS AND HIERARCHIES

Intercommunity relations continue to plague refugee communities; with scarce resources and prized resettlement places at a premium, it often seems like a zero-sum game between even closely related groups. Thus, internal tensions exist even within ethnic categories, as illustrated by debates over naming conventions. One Hakha Chin interlocutor remarked: "Zomi sound funny to Mizo people, so they make fun of them. We're all people of Zo [*mi* means people], so Mi-zo and Zo-mi mean the same thing. We're all Chin, but Zomi want to be different" (fieldwork interview 2015). More concerning are inter-ethnic attitudes among refugee communities. One recorded comment demonstrates such problematic perceptions: "Rohingya—they are primitive, I pity them. The first time I met them was in India, and they were illiterate and poor, camping outside the UNHCR office in Delhi and making the area dirty; that caused some problems." Such attitudes show how educational background and perceived cultural sophistication create supposed hierarchies that affect both community relations and individual opportunities (Brees 2010).

The differential treatment these communities experience within Malaysia and international resettlement systems and the perceived statuses of refugee groups, either among each other or from the point of view of service providers, show how religious identity, education, and perceived integration potential continue to shape refugee experiences. While both groups have established significant populations in Malaysia, their prospects remain uncertain and dependent on Malaysian government policies, international resettlement opportunities, and political developments in Myanmar (Hoffstaedter 2017a; Hoffstaedter and Jalil 2025). These uncertainties that refugees navigate through place-making strategies and community-building activities are examined in subsequent chapters. Understanding these migration patterns and settlement experiences provides crucial insights into contemporary displacement dynamics in Southeast Asia. The sophisticated organizational structures these communities have developed also demonstrate refugee agency and innovation in navigating precarious legal status, challenging victimization narratives, and highlighting the resourcefulness of displaced populations in creating new forms of belonging and security within hostile policy environments, resourcefulness that forms the foundation for the detailed ethnographic analysis that follows in subsequent chapters.

CHAPTER 2

Hospitality Toward Refugees in Malaysia

Religion, Culture, and Identity

Malaysia has a mixed track record in providing refuge to people seeking sanctuary and hospitality. This chapter charts a history of Malaysia's refugee engagement, mainly based on shared regional cultural and/or religious affiliations. I argue that the recent Malaysian history of refugee treatment presents a case for Muslim solidarity, but one tempered by a prevalent racism in Malaysia against people from the Indian subcontinent. Civil society also operates within religious and ethnic confines directed by the state, refugees themselves, and civil society actors. This chapter traces Chin and Rohingya refugees' engagement with Malaysian hospitality, deploying Derrida's (2000) conceptualization of hospitality to situate them within the Malaysian socio-political terrain and to draw out the possibilities and limits of such an approach.

Malaysia's social contract and its creation of an "us and them" paradigm reveal the foundation upon which all forms of hospitality, conditional or otherwise, rest in contemporary Malaysia. The informal agreement following independence in the late 1950s was that non-Malays would be granted citizenship and naturalized, and in exchange, Malays would receive concessions on several fronts, establishing the template for conditional inclusion that continues to shape refugee experiences today. Islam became the religion of the federation, and the Malay rulers became heads of state, heads of Islam in their respective states, and took over the British High Commissioner's role of protecting the rights and privileges of Malays and other indigenous peoples. These protections and privileges included quota systems for the civil service,

Malay land reserves, and scholarships. The Reid Commission, which drafted the constitution, wanted these privileges to remain after independence since a sudden withdrawal would have caused hardship, but suggested a review of these terms after fifteen years. However, there has never been a review. The ethnically based quota system put in place at independence remains in effect to this day.

The social contract, never formalized, remained an open-ended exchange following independence, creating ambiguities that continue to affect how refugees navigate Malaysian society. The lack of clarity on what the social contract entailed has left the constitutional bargain vulnerable to political interpretation, and "no nation can be securely grounded if the founding charter of its existence is confused or contested" (Puthucheary 2008, 27). In order to "share the nation," Norani Othman et al. (2008) argue that the ambiguities inherent in such a vague contract must be talked about in a mutual and cooperative spirit. However, such aims are far from being realized in the present climate.

In 1969, Malaysia's simmering ethnic tensions exploded in racial riots in Kuala Lumpur, with ensuing violence across the peninsula, establishing the traumatic reference point that today continues to constrain political discourse and refugee acceptance. The 1969 election was fought over sensitive issues of education and language, and it resulted in political upheaval (Andaya and Andaya 2001, 297). In the May 10 federal elections, voters abandoned the Alliance (UMNO, MCA, and MIC)[1] in favor of non-Malay parties such as the Democratic Action Party (DAP) and *Parti Gerakan Rakyat Malaysia*, while the Malay-based Islamist party *Parti Islam Se-Malaysia* (PAS) made deep incursions into the Malay vote. To curb the violence, the government called a state of emergency that lasted until 1971 and implemented far-reaching Malay affirmative action policies, most notably the New Economic Policy (NEP), to boost Malay ownership of the Malaysian economy. The NEP provided a legal framework for Malay positive discrimination, understood as compensation for the Malays sharing "their" country with others.

1 The Alliance (*Parti Perikatan*) was a coalition consisting of the United Malays National Organization (UMNO), Malaysian Chinese Association (MCA), and Malaysian Indian Congress (MIC).

HOSPITALITY AND ITS CONDITIONS

It is into this contested political backdrop that refugees walk when they arrive in Malaysia. "Hospitality" has a multitude of meanings, usually denoting the offering of a place to rest before moving on. Yet in the Malaysian context, who has the right to offer hospitality? What kind of hospitality is possible in a highly contested nation, where its own citizens are sometimes deemed guests? According to Derrida (2000), there is something subversive inherent in hospitality: *Hospitalité* and *hostilité* (hostility) are two sides of the same coin, pointing to "the control and management of strangers and the danger they embody" (Rozakou 2015, 565). This is Derrida's "aporia of hospitality": in order to host, one must be in control of the home. The host has power over the guest, yet hospitality is about giving it all away to the stranger, being open to the other in a way that shares everything with them, creating the fundamental tension that underlies all refugee-host relationships in Malaysia.

In the first instance, the host creates borders and boundaries, so that an inside and an outside are visible and readily intelligible, allowing all to see where the host may host and the guest be the guest. Second, the impossible hospitality, according to Derrida, opens up the home to everyone seeking a place to stay, relinquishing all control, thereby diminishing the possibility of hosting. This makes Derrida's hospitality and its inherent tensions reminiscent of Mauss's gift ([1954] 2002) and the obligations that come from it; indeed, Derrida's own conception of the gift is akin to this, in that the impossible gift must not grant the giver any power over the recipient. Here, Derrida highlights an etymological connection between hospitality and hostility: the word "hospitality" derives from *hospes*, which is linked to *hostis*, an earlier term that carried the dual meaning of both stranger and enemy. The concept of hospitality thus emerged from *hostilis* (stranger/enemy) combined with *potes* (having power), originally signifying the host's power over the stranger or enemy. This power dynamic is inherent to hospitality: the host necessarily determines the conditions under which the stranger's needs and comforts are met. Beyond merely setting these boundaries, Derrida argues that the host's authority stems fundamentally from their ownership of the space or place being shared. Since hospitality requires prior ownership before it can be extended to another, it contains an intrinsic structural tension. There is also the risk, as Dawson (2014, 83) notes, of people positioning themselves "as hotel guests with privileges rather than citizens with responsibilities." Thus, the possible and impossible hospitality are in constant ethical and political tension. Hospitality is always dangerous, e.g., what if the guests take over, or change the host society? Indeed, this fear is often picked up by the media in its coverage of immigration, refugee resettlement, and asylum debates.

In the Australian refugee debates, former Prime Minister John Howard is remembered for his statement, "We will decide who comes to this country and ... [under what] circumstances ... ." Before this infamous quote, however, he said:

> It's about this nation saying to the world we are a generous open hearted people taking more refugees on a per capita basis than any nation except Canada, we have a proud record of welcoming people from 140 different nations. But we will decide who comes to this country and the circumstances in which they come. (Howard 2001)

Thus, Howard precisely encapsulated the tension inherent in hosting guests and maintaining sovereignty, demonstrating the calculated nature of hospitality that shapes refugee experiences across different national contexts. Most countries deal with this in different ways: some portray a more or less friendly openness to the outside world, while others try to scare people off while maintaining other forms of hospitality, such as guest-worker schemes, refugee resettlement, and immigration. Therefore, hospitality is in a constant process of negotiation; it "has to be reinvented at every second, it is something without a pre-given rule" (Derrida 2000).

In Malaysia, many Malays see themselves in a state of continued tension with non-Malays (or rather non-*bumiputeras*), and this is often framed as hospitality toward *pendatang*, or newcomers, be they Chinese, Indian, Burmese, refugees, Indonesian, or others. This framing of otherness and inside versus outside within national discourse effectively places people into ethnic categories from which they cannot escape. Born into one such category, it becomes destiny, and difficult to circumvent the politics it encapsulates. This holds especially for people of mixed backgrounds; newcomers into this volatile, ethnically delineated body politic have to choose an identity or be placed within existing matrices. Hyphenated or creole identities are not tenable in Malaysia, especially when Islam is involved.

Rohingya refugees, because of their appearance and language, are placed within the Bangladeshi migrant worker category and may find a temporary place within society as a marginalized undocumented worker, alongside those often labeled with the derogatory term "Bangla." Chin refugees, because of their features, can more easily blend in and find refuge in predominantly Chinese neighborhoods. Here they are guests of Chinese hosts, who often employ them, rent houses to them, and on occasion socialize with them. However, with nationalist Malay politicians calling Chinese Malaysians *pendatang*, their ability to host is also questioned, revealing the fragile nature of hospitality that extends even to established ethnic minorities.

Derrida (2000, 149) wants us "to intervene in the condition of hospitality in the name of the unconditional." For him, hospitality is ethics, and ethics is hospitality: it is "culture itself and not simply one ethic amongst others." It requires transgressing self-identity and being vulnerable to the other and at their mercy, which are preconditions that rely on the belief in the underlying goodness of the human condition. This is far removed from our dominant realities in our present time, and the limitations in Malaysia are precisely an inability of many people to move beyond their self-ascribed and state-provided identity categories and welcome not just the stranger, but another version of themselves.

And yet, it is here where the hope lies: in the personal practice of hospitality. The nation, the state, and the government are constructs that depend on clear boundaries—the categories of inside and outside, citizen and non-citizen. Individuals have more capacity to dream and the flexibility to conceive of a spectrum, rather than binaries. Thus, they can be hospitable and live the ethics in everyday life, in spite of the nation and in ignorance of the government and its policies. One Rohingya refugee offered this differentiated view of discrimination in Malaysia:

> The Rohingya are discriminated by law, by the government, not by people, general people [...] they're very polite.... When they go rent the house, the general people, they never say anything. "Ok, you're Rohingya, can. Just pay my rent." That's all. That's sympathy. (Rohingya interlocutor, fieldwork interview, February 13, 2017)

On a sunny afternoon, I met a Malay man, Mohammad, at a Rohingya madrasah. He was helping paint the school and providing general updates to a modest, old building at the edge of town. Mohammad was not a political person; he neither expressed a political will to change the government's stance on refugees nor was he aware of what that stance was at present. He had heard about the local Rohingya population being in need of support and had volunteered. He knew that the Rohingya were from Myanmar and that life there was very hard for them. Thus, he offered to help. There was no underlying humanitarian idealism beyond the human recognition of another's need and the ability to help. He was living proof of Derrida's unconditional hospitality, in his lived experience of offering himself to the other, without need for recognition of his superiority or sovereignty, demonstrating the individual compassion that enables survival despite structural hostility.

In talking with him, I noticed that he was quite religious, and I asked him whether he was helping the Rohingya as fellow Muslims and whether their shared religion was what motivated his humanitarianism. He winced: "No. I am doing this because they are in need." Had he helped other, non-Muslim refugees? "No, I don't know any. But I would, if I did." This is another boundary of the openness I lamented earlier. It may be true that Mohammad would have helped anyone, but because of his Malaysian upbringing in times of accelerated Islamization and Malay nationalist agendas, he mostly knew Malays, socialized with Malays, and generally interacted with Malays. In his everyday life, Malayness was the norm, and the inclusion of Rohingya refugees constituted a closer ethno-religious bond than with fellow Malaysians, such as predominantly Hindu Indian-Malaysians or majority Buddhist Chinese-Malaysians. Thus, his hospitality-ethics may be interpreted not as unconditional, but premised on the conditionality of a shared cultural, religious bond that made Rohingya understandable to him and akin to him, revealing the cultural boundaries that shape even the most generous expressions of hospitality. Such a cultural matrix also played out for another Rohingya refugee who recounted how Malay landlords sometimes provided protection against workplace exploitation:

> I rented a room from the Malay and Malay is an old man and I went to the Malay, "Pak cik: I have this problem. This Chinese guy is not paying me".... And he directly took action against the Chinese. Even he called to the Chinese, "If you don't pay his salary, today I will make a report against you." Automatically he paid. (Rohingya interlocutor, fieldwork interview, February 13, 2017)

On another occasion, I had the opportunity to accompany a Christian Chinese Malaysian businessman in his 50s on one of his rounds throughout the Klang Valley, distributing food items to Chin families. Joseph regularly traveled around 100 km from his house to several suburbs and towns where he knew Chin families in need of additional rice, oil, and baby supplies. He got to know these families through his church network, which shares information with a Chin fellowship church and refugee organization about needy recipients. With the help of volunteers from his church, Joseph undertook weekly aid runs, but on this occasion, it was just the two of us in a four-wheel drive filled with supplies.

When I asked him about his motivations for helping Chin refugees in Malaysia, he told me that they have no one to help them, neither the government nor the UNHCR. Thus, it is up to individuals like him to support the poor and needy. I asked about the cultural and religious affinity he shares with Chin refugees—a shared Christian identity—but he rebuffed the insinuation: "I help because there is a need." Joseph, too, believes in the universal humanitarian principles on which Mohammad framed his aid for the Rohingya. Yet, in both cases, their belief in this unconditional and universal principle was tempered by the Malaysian straitjacket of their cultural and religious backgrounds. Chin refugee organizations and churches have virtually no contact with Muslim/Malay organizations or people, apart from instrumental contacts at the police and immigration to pay bribes more effectively. They seek out and receive help mostly from Chinese businesses, churches, and welfare organizations, revealing the ethnic and religious boundaries that structure even the most generous expressions of hospitality. But even this seemingly obvious connection is complicated by Malaysian political realities. For example, some Christian churches actively support Christian refugees by offering their churches as venues for refugee church services, community centers, or group activities. Yet others, especially smaller denominations, have been more wary of associating themselves with refugees. A friend of mine, a Chin who belonged to a minority Christian denomination, took me to a service at his church above a shop lot in Pudu, and we discussed the issue of refugees with his pastor. I remarked that the Malaysian headquarters of their denomination was a short distance away. They smiled and replied that they knew, and had in fact reached out for support from their brethren, but were disappointed when the Malaysian pastor told them that the government was already watching them and they could not afford to be seen as supporting an "illegal refugee community." Nonetheless, my refugee friend and his pastor bore no ill will toward them—they appreciated that the Malaysian congregation, as a minority of a minority in Malaysia, i.e., a Christian minority denomination within a predominantly Islamic country, was in a somewhat precarious situation.

In academia, like in real life, hospitality remains a contested notion. We talk about our good deeds, our achievements, while we are haunted by our failings and the violence we perpetrate against others. In Malaysia, traffickers and immigration officials continue to profit from the cross-border smuggling of people in search of hospitality. Derrida reminds us of the inner struggle, the inner tension, between ethics and politics, between what is possible and desirable, between what is feasible and what is right. The state and its agents, for the most part, make a show of overcoming this struggle by trumpeting their achievements and downplaying their failures of hospitality. In their eyes, hospitality is the sovereign state's prerogative and is measured by a movable target of successes and failures. In Malaysia, the inner contradictions of citizenship and inclusion in the body politic remain unresolved, suspended in a toxic mix of emotions, rewritten history, and uncertain futures. Thus, our only recourse is hospitality as an entirely human endeavor and practice of all of us here today, whether in the suburbs of Kuala Lumpur, San Francisco, or Sydney.

RELIGIOUS SOLIDARITY AND ITS LIMITS

Malaysia's Islamic identity and membership in the Organization of Islamic Cooperation have generated expectations among Muslim refugees that shared religious affiliation might facilitate integration or, at a minimum, spur the provision of community support through mosques and Islamic organizations. The reality, however, reveals how ethnic and national origin override religious solidarity, particularly for African Muslim refugees whose phenotypic difference marks them as fundamentally "other" despite sharing the Islamic faith with the Malay majority.

The experience of Mahad and his Somali family offers painful clarity into these dynamics. I met them as they were experiencing financial difficulty living in an outer suburb of Kuala Lumpur, where older, low-set housing estates from the 1970s and 80s stand interspersed with commercial lots, food stalls, and car repair shops. In such areas, ongoing development displaces plantations and the formerly wild fringes of the metropolis. We were led up to the second floor of the building where the family lives, then up another flight of stairs to a makeshift Somali refugee community school and meeting room. Settling in to hear their story, the contrast between expectation and reality became immediately apparent.

Mahad, the patriarch and chairperson of the local Somali community, arrived in Kuala Lumpur in 2007 as a former sales manager with Somali Airlines. His professional background suggested skills and experience that might translate into Malaysian employment, yet after over 15 years in the country, no one in his family of seven, including the two children born in Malaysia, currently had a job. "None of them can find work; they have been looking for work, but without luck," I was told. One family member worked briefly on an oil palm plantation but was cheated out of his paycheck, an experience that revealed both the exploitation facing refugees and their limited recourse against such treatment.

FIGURE 5 Home altar in a Chin refugee household for maintaining religious identity in displacement

The family now relied entirely on remittances from relatives resettled in Canada, creating a transnational dependency that highlights the failure of local integration despite years of residence in Malaysia. This family's near-permanent state of unemployment stands in stark contrast to other refugee populations, such as Chin finding work in restaurants and construction and Rohingya in markets and kitchens, suggesting a systematic rather than incidental exclusion.

Fatimah, Mahad's wife, attempted to become an entrepreneur with UNHCR support in 2010. The agency assisted her in establishing a business making Somali food, recognizing both her culinary skills and the potential market among diaspora communities. She successfully set up her stall in the UNHCR compound to demonstrate the viability of her food preparation. However, expanding the business elsewhere proved impossible due to systematic exclusion from Malaysian commercial spaces.

The problem, as Fatimah explained, was finding a market for her food beyond the UNHCR compound. She tried the local *masjid* (mosque), believing that Islamic spaces might welcome Muslim entrepreneurs regardless of national origin. The imam, however, turned her away, not only for regular business but even for the Ramadan market, when vendors from rural areas typically travel to the city to sell specialty foods. This rejection carried a particular sting given Ramadan's emphasis on charity, community, and breaking bread together across social boundaries. If Muslim solidarity cannot manifest even during Islam's holiest month, its practical limitations become all too obvious.

Both Mahad and Fatimah are practicing Muslims who had hoped that Malaysia's Muslim-majority status and history of providing sanctuary to Muslim refugees might translate into concrete support from local Muslim populations. As they explained with evident disappointment, racism in Malaysia has made it extremely hard for African refugees to find work. The discrimination operates at multiple levels, e.g., employers refuse to hire them, customers avoid their businesses, landlords charge premium rates or refuse to rent altogether, and even religious institutions that theoretically champion Islamic brotherhood maintain exclusionary practices.

The racialization of African refugees into a category fundamentally separate from Malaysian Muslims, despite shared religious practice, despite years of residence, and despite professional qualifications, reveals how looking different trumps religious faith in determining belonging. Malays often call Rohingya refugees "Bangla" due to physical appearance, racializing them as temporary foreign workers despite religious commonality. But this misidentification at least places the Rohingya within imaginable categories of belonging, as Bangladeshis are familiar South Asian migrants. African refugees, by contrast, fit no existing Malaysian categories and thus experience exclusion of a different magnitude.

African refugee communities, mostly small populations from Sudan and Somalia, have been most profoundly affected by this racialized exclusion.

Many fled the long civil war in Somalia beginning in 1991 and particularly following violent clashes in 2006. As comparatively recent arrivals, their community organizations lack the infrastructure and networks that Chin or Rohingya organizations have developed over decades. They face constant harassment and the effects of systematic racism that takes precedence over their Muslim identity.

Whereas Chin refugees can often blend into Chinese neighborhoods and Rohingya into Malay or Bangladeshi areas, Somali and Sudanese refugees stand out wherever they live, making them easy targets for local thugs and enforcement agencies alike. This visibility without acceptance creates a particularly vulnerable position. A conversation with a Sudanese refugee from Darfur further illustrated these dynamics. He had been in Malaysia since 2007—the same year as Mahad—and had similarly never found employment despite persistent searching. "Malaysians see us as Africans, our reputation is not so good," he explained with weary resignation. His gestures towards other Sudanese refugees standing nearby emphasized the collective nature of this exclusion, i.e., it was not individual failure but systematic marginalization. "The only jobs available are those in the small Sudanese community in Kuala Lumpur," he said. Then, summarizing with devastating brevity, he said, "It is a very miserable situation."

The failure of Islamic solidarity to transcend racial boundaries exposes important limitations in Malaysia's self-presentation as a Muslim nation open to co-religionists. Mosques have not been as accommodating toward African refugees as churches have been toward Christian refugees, in part because Malaysian mosques lack the tradition and infrastructure that some Christian churches have developed for refugee support. But this infrastructural explanation obscures a deeper reality: even when non-Malaysian Muslims pray in Malaysian mosques, the discrimination they face in employment, housing, and daily interactions reveals that shared religious practice cannot overcome racialized exclusion.

Rohingya Muslims pray in Malaysian mosques, attend Quranic classes, and participate in religious festivals alongside Malays, yet still experience marginalization and economic precarity. African Muslims face even more severe exclusion, suggesting a hierarchy of acceptability based on proximity to Malaysian ethnic and cultural norms. Bosnian refugees, lighter-skinned and European, have experienced relatively easier integration despite being Muslim minorities. Cham refugees from Cambodia and Vietnam, with cultural and linguistic connections to Malay civilization, similarly find greater acceptance. The pattern shows that "Islamic solidarity" in practice operates through filters of race, culture, and civilizational proximity that determine who counts as a deserving co-religionist (Hoffstaedter 2017b).

The prevalent societal racism that structures these exclusions reflects both historical patterns and contemporary anxieties. Malaysian attitudes toward South Asians remain colored by colonial-era labor importation and persistent stereotypes about Indian and Bangladeshi workers. These prejudices extend to the Rohingya despite their distinct identity, as their physical appearance triggers associations with unwelcome migrant labor. African refugees face additional layers of prejudice rooted in global anti-Black racism, stereotypes about African poverty and instability, and unfamiliarity that breeds suspicion.

For Mahad, Fatimah, and the Sudanese refugee, Malaysia's Islamic identity promised refuge and potential belonging. Instead, they discovered that the Muslim brotherhood has strict racial and cultural limits, that professional skills cannot overcome phenotypic differences, and that years of residence engender neither integration nor acceptance. Their bitter disappointment reflects not naive expectations, but reasonable hopes based on Islamic teachings about the *ummah* (global Muslim community) and Malaysia's rhetorical commitments to helping Muslim refugees. The disconnect between rhetoric and reality extends to government policy. Malaysian officials occasionally speak out about Muslim refugee crises, e.g., condemning Myanmar's treatment of Rohingya, but these statements do not translate into domestic policy changes. Rhetorical performances of Islamic solidarity generate goodwill in international forums while doing little for refugees actually residing in Malaysia. The result is a peculiar dynamic where Malaysia presents itself as champion of Muslim refugees abroad while systematically marginalizing Muslim refugees within its borders (Hoffstaedter 2017b).

Thus, religion alone proves insufficient to generate hospitality or integration in contemporary Malaysia. Shared faith cannot overcome racial hierarchies, economic anxieties, or cultural unfamiliarity. For African Muslim refugees, Malaysia's Islamic identity creates expectations that Malaysia's racial politics systematically fail to fulfill, producing a particularly painful form of exclusion. Religion plays a particularly crucial role here, as it creates expectations but also offers both theological frameworks for assistance and practical networks for service delivery.

THE MUSLIM HOSPITALITY NETWORK

The Qur'anic precepts, along with Hadith and Sunnah that detail the Prophet's treatment of displaced peoples, demonstrate a clear historical and theological disposition toward providing refuge to those in need. These Islamic traditions offer rich resources for understanding obligations toward refugees that predate modern international law. However, contemporary Islamic nations, including those with Muslim majorities, have struggled to translate these theological commitments into practical legal frameworks or policy implementations, creating a gap between principle and practice that affects refugee experiences across multiple domains. Malaysia exemplifies this disconnect between religious principle and political practice. While the country is a signatory to the 1990 Cairo Declaration on Human Rights in Islam, adopted by the Organisation of Islamic Cooperation, the document's references to sharia law render it more aspirational than legally enforceable (Organisation of Islamic Cooperation 1990). Article 12 of the Cairo Declaration explicitly provides for the right to seek asylum from persecution, yet Malaysia's actual immigration policies contradict this commitment.

The fragmented nature of Malaysia's legal systems compounds this problem. Although Malaysia enforces sharia law, these regulations predominantly focus on personal status matters affecting only Muslims. Constitutional and federal matters, including immigration law, remain outside sharia jurisdiction, effectively severing Islamic precepts from refugee policy. This legal separation ensures that Islamic concepts of hospitality and protection have no bearing on how refugees are actually treated by the state. Despite these structural limitations, some progress has emerged at the state level. Governments and bureaucracies operate across multiple levels, and while international frameworks have gained little traction, Malaysian state governments and their institutions have begun exploring new approaches. State Islamic authorities, in particular, have started considering how to direct funds toward Muslim refugees. Recently, the muftis of Pahang and Kelantan issued significant opinions declaring that *zakat* (alms, one of the five pillars of Islam requiring Muslims to give portions of their wealth to the poor and needy) can be legitimately used to help refugees (Wan Syamsul Amly 2015). Although disagreements persist over which category of worthy recipients Rohingya refugees should occupy, these pronouncements carry considerable weight given that they come from learned Islamic scholars wielding substantial power within their respective state Islamic institutions.

Understanding how religion shapes refugee assistance in Malaysia requires grappling with Islam's complex and often divisive role in contemporary Malaysian politics (Hoffstaedter 2011a). Recent years have witnessed significant social and political unrest around such fundamental questions as, What role should Islam play in governance? Do Muslims enjoy genuine religious freedom? Can Christians legitimately use the Arabic word "Allah" in their Malay-language Bibles? These debates reflect deeper tensions about Malaysia's identity as a Muslim-majority nation, tensions that affect how refugees navigate religious networks and community support systems. The federal constitution grants Islam the status of "religion of the federation," yet extensive debate continues over this designation's practical implications. Scholars and politicians argue over whether this reflects the Reid Commission's original secular intentions or justifies a more expansive form of Islamic governance. The past several decades have witnessed the dramatic Islamization of state institutions and legal frameworks, fundamentally transforming how Islam is lived, performed, and taught throughout Malaysia (Liow 2009). Government funding now generously supports Islamic causes, while federal and state religious bureaucracies have expanded significantly, reshaping the religious landscape and creating new opportunities and constraints for refugee communities.

Malaysia's membership in the Organisation of Islamic Cooperation (OIC) reflects its aspirations to represent moderate Muslim principles on the international stage. Various prime ministers have declared Malaysia an Islamic state, often for polemical and political purposes. Yet, Islam undeniably plays a crucial role in contemporary Malaysian identity and how the majority of citizens understand themselves (Hoffstaedter 2011a). This Islamic identity creates potential for social and political mobilization around fellow Muslims in need. Government officials and Muslim NGOs regularly organize awareness campaigns and fundraising efforts for Palestinian causes and, more recently, Syrian civil war victims (Asmady Idris 2012). Charity galas, documentary films, and other fundraising activities consistently highlight Palestinian refugee suffering while Malaysia maintains its position as a vocal critic of Israeli policies and a strong supporter of Palestinian causes internationally. However, few of these activities result in meaningful governmental intervention and support for Rohingya refugees, exposing the selective nature of Islamic solidarity.

Malaysia's historical approach to refugee protection reveals how religious bonds intersect with other factors to determine who receives sanctuary. While shared Islamic faith emerges as one significant consideration, access to rights appears more strongly influenced by historical, cultural, and linguistic connections between Malays and particular refugee populations. The Malaysian government has consistently favored groups closely related to the Malay Peninsula through mobility patterns, cultural affinity, and linguistic compatibility. Thai Muslims from Southern Thailand, Cham refugees from Cambodia and Vietnam, and Acehnese from Indonesia all benefit from belonging to the greater Malay world, a connection where Islam now plays a major role, though not necessarily the defining one. The protection offered to Bosnian and Syrian refugees represents notable exceptions to this pattern of geographic and cultural proximity (Karčić 2014). In both cases, Malaysia provided sanctuary to geographically distant populations who could not otherwise reach Malaysia independently, thus avoiding the creation of additional pull factors that might encourage further refugee flows from these regions. These decisions also generated positive international headlines that projected Malaysia favorably on the world stage, rather than representing genuine engagement with refugee protection norms and practices.

Mahathir's use of Bosnian refugees proved particularly effective in shaming the international community's inadequate response to Muslim victims in the former Yugoslavia, while simultaneously raising Malaysia's profile as a leader in the moderate Islamic world. Similarly, Najib's pledge at the United Nations to accept Syrian refugees marked his engagement with an international crisis, though the relatively small numbers involved and the absence of regulatory frameworks for implementation revealed the limitations of such symbolic gestures (Mayberry 2015). Beyond these realpolitik considerations, Malaysia has nonetheless gained genuine experience in providing refuge to some distant fellow Muslims. Yet it remains striking that the Malaysian government continues to frame these humanitarian interventions in secular terms rather than invoking religious language or positioning Islam as an alternative or complementary framework to Western-centric refugee conventions, creating missed opportunities for more sustainable protection frameworks.

The secular framing that characterizes Malaysia's approach reflects and reinforces broader conceptual limitations in how refugees are understood and represented. For example, refugees are most commonly understood through what might be called a "deficiency model," or a framework that defines refugeeness as inherently denoting lack. This perspective assumes refugees arrive lacking status, money, legality, power, and agency, with these deficiencies explaining both their displacement and their need for protection. Such framing inevitably positions refugees as potential threats to local populations, assuming they will compete for jobs, welfare benefits, and tax resources in what becomes a zero-sum economic calculation. This deficiency model creates a conceptual trap where refugees can never transcend their status as charity cases, sources of cheap labor, or worthy recipients of goodwill and taxation (Harrell-Bond 1999). The framework prevents the recognition of refugees as complete human beings with skills, aspirations, and contributions to make, instead reducing them to their immediate needs and vulnerabilities. Breaking free from this model requires recognizing that displacement, while traumatic, does not erase human agency, capacity, or dignity.

The landscape of refugee assistance in Malaysia reflects broader constraints on civil society while revealing innovative adaptations by both local organizations and refugee communities themselves. Understanding who provides help, and who cannot, illuminates the complex intersection of political restrictions, ethnic boundaries, and religious networks that shape refugee experiences. Refugee assistance in Malaysia operates within a severely constrained civil society environment shaped by decades of government efforts to limit progressive organizations. This restrictive approach contrasts sharply with Malaysia's early post-independence period, when Giersdorf and Croissant (2011, 7) describe relatively relaxed governmental attitudes toward civil society between 1957 and 1969. The 1970s witnessed the emergence of universal human rights concerns, marked by the establishment of several women's and human rights organizations (Brown et al. 2004, 12; Case 2003, 46; Giersdorf and Croissant 2011, 8). The 1980s brought renewed tensions, particularly around Chinese Malaysian concerns focused on vernacular education, creating instability within the ruling Barisan Nasional coalition.

These mounting pressures culminated in Operation Lalang in 1987, a decisive police crackdown that fundamentally reshaped Malaysia's civil society landscape. The operation involved arresting over 100 activists and politicians under the Internal Security Act while temporarily banning several newspapers (Brown et al. 2004, 12; Giersdorf and Croissant 2011, 9). This systematic intimidation campaign established clear boundaries around acceptable civil society activities, with the government maintaining strict control over organizational registration while wielding Internal Security Act powers to detain individuals indefinitely without charge. The lasting impact of Operation Lalang continues to shape contemporary civil society. Many organizations now register as private companies to avoid regulatory constraints, while those that do operate as formal NGOs must navigate extensive legal restrictions. The amended federal constitution and Sedition Act designate numerous topics as "sensitive" and off-limits for public discussion, including "the status of Islam as the official religion," "the status and power of the Malay Rulers," and, of particular relevance for refugee work, "citizenship rights for non-Malays" (Brown et al. 2004, 6).

CIVIL SOCIETY, THE UNHCR, AND REFUGEES BETWEEN STATE AND COMMUNITY

Contemporary civil society organizations operate under heightened state surveillance and strictly controlled media environments, though internet platforms have created some space for alternative coverage of refugee issues with reduced bias. The government demonstrates specific hostility toward human rights organizations while showing more tolerance for charitable activities, creating incentives for service providers to avoid advocacy in favor of direct assistance. The scant NGO resources in Malaysia naturally focus primarily on domestic political and human rights issues. Tenaganita, one of the few organizations specifically addressing migrant and refugee rights, especially around labor rights, advocates with the UNHCR and serves as a conduit for refugee concerns, though tight budgets and staff shortages leave this work under-resourced. SUARAM, a human rights organization that also supports refugees, faces similar resource constraints. Their domestic human rights work frequently puts them in opposition to the government, which harasses them and limits their operations, creating a difficult environment for all refugee support work. This state pressure keeps progressive civil society focused on domestic battles, limiting the pool of service providers and UNHCR implementing partners. The shortage is exacerbated by strained relationships between some NGOs and the UNHCR, which often wants to minimize criticism of the Malaysian government to maintain good relations. Legal aid exemplifies this gap. While committed Bar Council lawyers advocate for individual refugees, no centralized organization provides comprehensive legal support. Asylum Access, which opened a small Kuala Lumpur office in 2014, addresses complex UNHCR asylum cases but also operates under severe resource constraints.

Refugees typically navigate this landscape through personal and community networks. For most refugees from Myanmar, this means their community refugee organization. These organizations, established along ethnic or national lines, can be substantial: the two largest Chin groups claim over 50,000 members, including both current Malaysian residents and resettled refugees. In 2007, ethnic minority groups from Myanmar created the Coalition of Burma Ethnics, Malaysia (COBEM) to coordinate information-sharing, resource pooling, and UNHCR interactions. COBEM includes the Kachin Refugee Committee (KRC), Organisation of Karenni Development (OKD), Malaysia Karen Organisation (MKO), Chin Refugee Committee (CRC) with Alliance of Chin Refugees (ACR), Mon Refugee Organisation (MRO), Arakan Refugee Relief Committee (ARRC), and Shan Refugee Organisation

(SRO). As the best-organized refugee entity in Malaysia, representing for a long time the majority of refugees, COBEM maintains a good working relationship with the UNHCR, which has encouraged other refugee groups to replicate this model, finding it easier to work through a single legitimate representative organization per refugee ethnic or religious group.

Each community organization runs programs aimed at improving members' living and working conditions. Some maintain extensive employer networks across factories, restaurants, and plantations, quickly and efficiently placing newly arrived refugees in workplaces. They often review workplace agreements and mediate employer complaints from refugee workers, providing sophisticated services spanning employment, shelter, schools for children, and adult training facilities. UNHCR grants, diaspora donations, and membership fees fund these programs. Employed refugees typically pay around RM 50 (USD 13) for membership cards, which are often an asylum seeker's first form of identification and offer modest protection. Many organizations also charge monthly fees. Most other refugee groups lack this level of organization and offer only membership cards and a limited suite of services, depending on funding and the leadership's expertise. The success of many of these organizations has relieved pressure on UNHCR's limited resources but has complicated their relationships. Refugee community organizations depend on the UNHCR for registration but little else, running their own education, employment, and health programs, often partnering with Malaysian NGOs and UNHCR implementing partners. As organizations mature and develop effective leadership, they increasingly hold the UNHCR accountable, demanding improved services. A Chin Refugee Committee survey, for instance, reported slow, unprofessional, and inadequate UNHCR support in 2012 (Chin Refugee Committee 2013, 49).

Despite these constraints, refugee assistance emerges through three primary service categories, each shaped by distinct organizational capacities and religious networks. Healthcare services operate primarily through religious NGOs, though some have faced closure when church leaders grew concerned about government reprisal. International health organizations like Médecins Sans Frontières provide additional medical support, while local health NGOs and clinics offer intermittent outreach to both remote and urban communities, sometimes partnering with universities. Psychosocial support comes mainly through international expatriate and domestic networks of physicians, psychologists, and empathetic supporters, while the Taiwan Buddhist Tzu Chi Foundation is one of the few non-Christian religious organizations providing health services, creating a diverse but fragmented support landscape that refugees must navigate.

Educational services depend almost entirely on refugee community organizations established with UNHCR assistance and sustained through substantial support from local and expatriate volunteers. These schools operate in legal gray areas, constantly vulnerable to closure, while providing essential services that the Malaysian state refuses to offer directly. Livelihood support combines limited UNHCR pilot projects with extensive self-organization by refugee communities and arrangements with local and foreign labor brokers who supply workers to Malaysian businesses and industries. The effectiveness of these employment networks often depends on community organizations' relationships with employers and their capacity to advocate for fair treatment.

The success of service provision across all three categories depends fundamentally on refugee identity, specifically their religion, race, and ethnicity, and how these characteristics relate to existing political, cultural, and social networks within Malaysia. This creates a clear hierarchy of access that reflects and reinforces Malaysia's ethnic and religious boundaries rather than transcending them.

The practical implications of religious and ethnic networks become clear when examining specific refugee communities. Rohingya refugees benefit from connections to Malay Muslim networks, including individual supporters like Mohammad and organizations such as ABIM (Muslim Youth Movement), which has engaged directly with the Rohingya community needs. Madrasahs serve as crucial community centers, providing not only religious education but also social infrastructure for activities, meetings, and channels for support from the broader Muslim community, including Malaysian Muslims. During religious festivals like Eid al-Fitr, these institutions become focal points for charitable giving and community solidarity.

Chin refugees, by contrast, access support primarily through refugee community networks, which are usually based on ethno-religious identities. As described above, Chin are divided into smaller ethno-linguistic and religious groups that have created their own community organizations to serve their extended kin networks and co-ethnics. One example is the ACR, which operates a health clinic. These clinics are sometimes managed by expatriate professionals, such as Australian nurses, and tap into international fundraising networks within largely Western expatriate communities. The geographic and cultural distance of these support networks from local Malaysian politics provides some advantages, though it also reinforces Chin refugees' broader separation from Malaysian society.

There is a fundamental tension between ethical aspirations and the political realities of hospitality, philanthropy, and social welfare provision for refugees in Malaysia. Philanthropic and social welfare provisions largely depend on people recognizing need while feeling sufficiently invested to seek solutions. Yet in Malaysia, where diverse societal groups compete for limited resources and attention, the provision of services, support, and funding operates according to complex hierarchies determined by legal status, ethnic identity, and religious affiliation, which shape all aspects of the refugee experience.

Refugees find themselves systematically relegated to the margins of worthy recipients, their unresolved legal status ensuring they remain categorized alongside the broader population of undocumented migrants who face heavy policing, systematic discrimination, and barriers to establishing durable homes in Malaysia. This marginalization persists as long as the government maintains its refusal to recognize refugees as a distinct category deserving protection, leaving them trapped within the expansive "illegal immigrant" designation that justifies their exclusion from rights and services. Yet, my ethnographic research in the Klang Valley demonstrates how individual circumstances, including class background, educational attainment, entrepreneurial capacity, personal initiative, and simple fortune, significantly shape refugee experiences within these structural constraints. The unpredictable nature of assistance means that a chance encounter on the street can transform someone's prospects permanently, for better or worse. While membership in strong community networks provides important advantages, it cannot guarantee access to better services, resources, or aid. For all refugees, the next step toward recognition and potential resettlement is registration with the UNHCR through the long and arduous process of becoming a refugee.

CHAPTER 3
Becoming a Refugee in Malaysia

INTRODUCTION: NAVIGATING LEGAL LIMBO

The process of becoming a refugee extends far beyond the administrative moment of status recognition. In Malaysia, a non-signatory state to the 1951 Refugee Convention, this transformation occurs within a complex web of bureaucratic procedures, community networks, and existential negotiations that fundamentally reshape individual identity and social belonging. For the thousands of displaced persons who arrive in Malaysia each year, primarily from Myanmar, the journey from asylum seeker to recognized refugee represents not merely a legal transition but a profound ontological shift that establishes the precarious foundation upon which all their subsequent experiences rest.

This chapter examines the bureaucratic and social processes through which individuals navigate the transformation from displaced persons to UNHCR-registered refugees in Malaysia's unique legal landscape. Drawing on extensive ethnographic data from UNHCR registration interviews and community interactions, I analyze the manifold challenges refugees face in proving ethnic identity without documentation, the crucial role of community organizations in accessing protection, and the ways in which "becoming" a refugee encompasses dimensions of existence that far exceed legal recognition (cf. Malkki 1995b). The theoretical framework for understanding this transformation draws upon several interconnected concepts. Heidegger's notion of being-in-the-world provides insight into how refugees experience existential displacement and the search for authentic existence within hostile environments (Heidegger 1962; see also Young 2002). Deleuze's concept of becoming offers a dynamic understanding of identity formation that moves beyond fixed categories to embrace the fluid, processual nature of refugee subjectivity (Deleuze and Guattari 1987; Nail 2015). However, while these philosophical frameworks explicate the transformative potential inherent in displacement, the lived reality of refugees in Malaysia often involves what Agamben (1998) terms "bare life," i.e., an existence stripped of political significance and reduced to biological survival.

Yet as Dunn and Cons (2013) demonstrate in their pioneering work on refugee camps, Agamben's framework of "homo sacer" proves insufficient for understanding the complex agency that refugees exercise even within severely constrained circumstances (see also Owens 2010; Turner 2016). Their concept of "aleatory sovereignty"—rule by contingency—better captures how refugees navigate unpredictable bureaucratic systems where chance plays a commanding role in determining life outcomes (cf. Sigona 2014). In Malaysia's context, where refugees exist in legal limbo without formal state recognition, this contingent sovereignty becomes particularly pronounced (Nah 2007).

THE REGISTRATION IMPERATIVE: DOCUMENTATION AND THE SPATIAL POLITICS OF PROTECTION

Before a refugee can be a refugee, they must undergo what emerges as a highly scripted process of becoming: registration with UNHCR Malaysia. However, this legalistic framework betrays the predominance of ordered documentation that defines contemporary statecraft, where passports enable travel, birth certificates confirm identity, and citizenship status provides the basis for claiming rights and accountability from the state. These represent fantasies of bureaucratic order for most refugees, who have fled precisely because core aspects of their being, such as their ethnicity, religion, political beliefs, or social status, were weaponized against them by the very states meant to protect them. For most refugees who arrive stateless, without birth records or travel documents, registration with UNHCR embodies a becoming that far exceeds simple administrative status change from asylum seeker to recognized refugee. For UNHCR registration officers, the process of status determination according to established rules and regulations becomes for refugees an embodiment of all potential futures, including the transformative possibility of resettlement that could radically alter their life trajectories and open new possibilities (Hoffstaedter and Lamb 2019).

This process unfolds within a hostile environment of rent-seeking, exclusion, and systematic discrimination. Malaysia's national immigration policy, based on the Immigration Act, heavily penalizes border crossings without relevant documentation through monetary fines up to RM 10,000 (USD 2,500), imprisonment up to five years, and corporal punishment of up to six strokes of the cane (Commissioner of Law Revision 2006). Within this punitive framework, refugees experience what can be characterized as profound ontic insecurity[1], or a fundamental uncertainty about one's very existence and place in the world that extends beyond immediate physical safety to encompass questions of identity, belonging, and future possibility (cf. Kinnvall 2004).

The UNHCR compound in Kuala Lumpur embodies the spatial politics of refugee recognition in Malaysia. Located atop a hill in an affluent inner-city neighborhood, surrounded by high metal fences and guarded by security personnel, the compound's very architecture communicates the hierarchical relationship between refugees and the international humanitarian apparatus meant to protect them. The juxtaposition is striking: next door stands the *Rumah Perkasa*, residence of the chief of Malaysia's armed forces, while the surrounding area features private schools and embassies. No public transport serves this area, forcing refugees to arrive by expensive taxi or, if they take the monorail, to walk 15 minutes and cross multiple dual carriageways. This spatial configuration is no accident. The compound's location reinforces refugees' marginal status while ensuring their separation from Malaysian society (cf. Darling 2016). The physical effort required to reach the compound, i.e., the expense, the dangerous road crossings, the climb up the hill, all serve as an initial filter that demonstrates the commitment required for recognition

1 I use "ontic security" rather than the more common "ontological security" deliberately, though the two terms are closely connected. The distinction derives from Heidegger's *Being and Time* (1962) where the *ontic* refers to the characteristics and properties of particular beings or entities (*das Seiende*), while the *ontological* refers to the structures that make beings intelligible as such, i.e., Being itself (*das Sein*). The ontological security tradition that runs from Laing (1960) through Giddens (1991), and into refugee, belonging and International Relations scholarship (see, e.g., Kinnvall 2004, Mitzen 2006, cf. Hage 1997 on home-building), adds a psychological register: ontological security then becomes a concept to describe a continuity of self-identity and a basic trust in the constancy of one's social and material world, intimately connected to a sense of belonging. My emphasis on the *ontic* here is to signal that for Chin and Rohingya refugees in Malaysia their elementary bare, legal and bodily sense of being is at stake, not just their structural in- or exclusion from society. Ontic insecurity, in this usage, names the condition in which a person's entity-status as someone-in-this-place is withheld by the state and its institutions. The two concepts are entangled in practice but separating them analytically helps account for why refugee place-making in Malaysia is at once existential and also material work.

while simultaneously marking refugees as supplicants seeking favor rather than individuals exercising rights (cf. Fassin 2012).

Indeed, one Rohingya refugee described the exhausting and repetitive nature of seeking UNHCR registration:

> The first time I came, they didn't allow me to go inside the UNHCR because they don't allow, they don't want to call you. The second time I went, I was able to go inside with my cousin, but they didn't accept.... After that I tried many times but they never call, they never call ... after thousand attempts. (Rohingya interlocutor, fieldwork interview July 17, 2017)

The compound itself consists of an old colonial bungalow housing the UNHCR administration, demountable structures accommodating implementing partner offices, and what staff colloquially term "the cage"—a large covered hall encompassing the main waiting area and air-conditioned registration buildings. This architectural metaphor proves apt: refugees enter an enclosed space where they await judgment on their claims while being physically separated from the administrative apparatus that will determine their fate. The atmosphere is charged with tension as refugees enter this space. Large fans move humid air around the open waiting hall, where hundreds of asylum seekers gather daily, hoping for news about their cases or attending scheduled interviews. The physical discomfort of intense heat, crowding, and long wait times creates an embodied experience of vulnerability and dependence, reinforcing the power dynamics inherent in the registration process.

MOHAMMAD'S STORY: PERFORMING REFUGEENESS

Mohammad's experience illustrates the complex psychological and social dimensions of becoming a refugee in Malaysia. A young Rohingya man who had fled Myanmar via Bangladesh, Mohammad approached his UNHCR status determination interview with a mixture of preparation and anxiety that reflects the high stakes involved in this bureaucratic encounter. The morning of his interview, Mohammad arrived at the UNHCR compound carrying no documents, ironically a circumstance that both strengthened and weakened his claim for protection. The people smugglers on his boat journey had confiscated and destroyed his papers, throwing them into the sea with the explanation that "it will be easier for you this way." This destruction of documentation, while traumatic, served the smugglers' interests by making it harder for authorities to trace routes and identify individuals for deportation. Yet Mohammad regretted this loss acutely, having heard that the UNHCR demands written evidence to verify refugee claims. This tension between the practical necessities of irregular migration and the bureaucratic requirements of formal protection systems creates a cruel paradox: the very processes that enable refugees to reach safety often destroy the evidence needed to secure legal recognition once they arrive.

Mohammad had attempted to prepare for his interview through community networks and information sessions. He attended a presentation organized by Asylum Access, an international legal NGO, where an intern explained UNHCR procedures and emphasized the importance of honesty and consistency for refugee testimonies. This preparation revealed both the sophistication of refugee information networks and their limitations. While Mohammad learned about procedural requirements, the session could not resolve fundamental challenges related to documentation, language barriers, and cultural translation. His friends counseled him strategically about interview content: "talk about the fighting," "and the discrimination," "and tell them how you couldn't go to university, even though your grades were so good." This advice reflected community knowledge about which narratives resonate with UNHCR decision-makers, but also highlighted the problematic requirement for refugees to perform their suffering in particular ways to gain recognition, performances that continue to shape how refugees present themselves in Malaysian society.

Mohammad's confidence that "everyone knows about Rohingya, so they have to let me in" demonstrated both reasonable expectations about international awareness of Rohingya persecution and naive assumptions about how bureaucratic systems actually function. The interview took place in an air-conditioned office within the compound, offering temporary respite from the heat and the crowds in the waiting area. This physical transition from discomfort to comfort marked the beginning of Mohammad's formal engagement with the status determination process. The registration officer, a Malaysian national with legal training, faced the daunting task of determining whether Mohammad's testimony warranted refugee protection. For Mohammad, this interview represented far more than an administrative review. It embodied all his hopes for a transformed future, including the possibility of resettlement to a third country where he might access education, employment, and security, something impossible in Malaysia. The officer's questions about his background, persecution experiences, and journey to Malaysia required Mohammad to construct a coherent narrative from traumatic memories while navigating language barriers and cultural differences.

The temporal dimensions of this encounter proved particularly complex. Mohammad needed to provide consistent details about events that occurred years earlier, during periods of extreme stress and trauma. Memory, particularly of traumatic events, rarely conforms to the linear, detailed narratives demanded by bureaucratic systems. The UNHCR's emphasis on consistency and chronological accuracy often conflicts with how human memory actually functions, especially under conditions of prolonged displacement and uncertainty (Cameron 2010). Thus, becoming a refugee requires not only surviving persecution and reaching safety, but also successfully performing victimhood in ways that satisfy bureaucratic requirements. This performance involves translating complex experiences of discrimination, violence, and displacement into categories recognizable to international protection systems. The gap between lived experience and administrative requirements can create additional trauma for individuals already struggling with the effects of persecution and displacement, trauma that continues to affect refugees' experiences of daily life in Malaysia.

PROVING ETHNIC IDENTITY: THE BURDEN OF AUTHENTICITY

The requirement that refugees prove their ethnic identity to qualify for protection creates further fundamental challenges that reveal the artificial nature of bureaucratic categories (cf. Scott 1998; Cohn 1996). For Rohingya and Chin refugees, demonstrating ethnic belonging becomes essential for accessing protection, yet this requirement contradicts the fluid, contextual nature of identity itself (Barth 1969; Wimmer 2008). Language serves as the primary marker of ethnic authenticity in UNHCR interviews, yet this test proves deeply problematic in practice (cf. Blommaert 2009; Maryns 2006). Registration officers, typically Malaysian nationals, cannot speak Rohingya or Chin languages and must rely on interpreters who are often refugees themselves. This creates conflicts of interest, as refugee interpreters may have personal connections, grudges, or competing interests that affect their translations (Inghilleri 2005; Pöllabauer 2004). The linguistic landscape proves more complex than simple ethnic categories suggest. Many Rohingya have lived in Bangladesh for years or decades, meaning their children may speak limited Rohingya or better Bengali than their putative "mother tongue" (Mohajan 2018). Village dialects, cross-border movements, and generational changes create additional complications for language-based identity verification (Eades 2010; Patrick 2012). An elderly Rohingya farmer from a remote village may speak a dialect incomprehensible to a younger interpreter from an urban area, calling into question who possesses authentic knowledge of "their" language. In addition, the availability of qualified interpreters creates challenges. Few Rohingya possess the education and English skills necessary to serve as professional interpreters, reflecting decades of educational exclusion in Myanmar. This shortage leads to longer waiting times, unprofessional behavior in interviews, and allegations of corruption as desperate refugees seek to influence the interpretation process.

Document-based verification proves equally problematic. Most refugees arrive without papers, having destroyed documents during flight, lost them to smugglers, or never possessed formal documentation due to statelessness. Those documents that survive often raise more questions than they answer. Myanmar government documents may not recognize ethnic categories claimed by refugees, while documents from refugee camps in Bangladesh may be inconsistent. The emphasis on consistency in testimony creates additional burdens for refugees who have experienced trauma, lengthy displacement journeys, and multiple interviewing processes. Memory, particularly of traumatic events, often proves unreliable on specific details while remaining vivid on emotional impacts. Refugees may provide different versions of events not because they are lying, but because memory itself is reconstructive rather than reproductive, challenges that affect not only bureaucratic encounters but also refugees' daily navigation of Malaysian society.

Due to overwhelming caseloads from Myanmar, UNHCR Malaysia has, for several years now, ceased accepting walk-in registrations; instead, refugees are required to join community organizations typically organized around ethnic identity and home-village connections within Myanmar (Hoffstaedter 2015; McConnachie 2018). This organizational requirement created new forms of dependency and control within refugee communities (cf. Harrell-Bond 1986, 1999; Kibreab 2004). Rather than approaching the UNHCR directly, displaced persons must first convince ethnic organizations of their authenticity and worthiness for support. This gatekeeping function gives community leaders significant power over individual refugee destinies, while creating opportunities for corruption, favoritism, and community conflict (Crisp 2002; Kaiser 2005).

The proliferation of refugee organizations reflects both community initiative and structural challenges. Multiple organizations may claim to represent the same ethnic group, leading to competition for members, resources, and UNHCR recognition. For Rohingya refugees, this multiplicity of organizations created particular challenges, as leadership squabbles and internecine conflicts have diminished community trust and complicated UNHCR partnership arrangements (Azis 2014; Wake and Cheung 2016). Contemporary practice sees UNHCR Malaysia working with only one recognized Rohingya organization, limiting refugee options for accessing registration and creating bottlenecks that delay status determination. This consolidation may improve administrative efficiency, but it reduces refugee agency and creates new vulnerabilities to organizational corruption or incompetence. The ethnic basis of refugee organization creates additional problems for individuals whose identities do not fit neat categories or who have inter-ethnic family connections. Mixed marriages, adoption across ethnic lines, or cultural assimilation may complicate organizational membership while creating questions about authentic ethnic belonging that can affect the chances of gaining protection access.

Community organizations provide essential services beyond UNHCR registration, including information sharing, emergency assistance, employment referrals, and social support. These services fill crucial gaps in Malaysia's non-signatory protection landscape, where refugees cannot access formal social services or employment rights. However, service provision by community organizations also institutionalizes refugees' dependence on ethnic networks rather than promoting integration into broader Malaysian society, a dependence that continues to shape their urban experiences. The requirement for organizational membership reinforces ethnic boundaries and identities that may have been fluid or contextual in their home communities. Refugees must perform ethnic authenticity not only for the UNHCR but also for community organizations whose leaders may have their own ideas about proper ethnic identity, cultural practice, or political loyalty. Generational conflicts within refugee organizations reflect broader tensions between maintaining connections to the homeland and adapting to Malaysian circumstances. Older leaders may emphasize traditional practices and return orientation, while younger members prioritize education, employment, and long-term settlement. These tensions affect organizational decision-making and service delivery, sometimes privileging particular groups within ethnic communities.

CREDIBILITY ASSESSMENT AND THE PRODUCTION OF TRUTH

Successfully navigating the UNHCR's specific registration requirements is paramount for refugees seeking protection. Its emphasis on credibility assessment reveals fundamental tensions between bureaucratic requirements for consistent evidence and the complex realities of refugee experience (cf. Coffey 2003; Herlihy et al. 2002). Registration officers rely on guidelines that prioritize internal consistency (coherence of testimony) and external consistency (agreement with known facts), while considering factors such as fluency, clarity, and detail in refugee narratives (UNHCR 2013; Sweeney 2009). This credibility framework assumes that truthful testimony will be consistent, detailed, and corroborated by external information sources. However, this assumption often conflicts with how memory functions, particularly for individuals who have experienced trauma, lengthy displacement journeys, and multiple interviewing processes (Rogers et al. 2015; Herlihy and Turner 2007). The demand for consistency may actually privilege coached testimony over authentic, but fragmented, memories of persecution and flight (Good 2007; Eastmond 2007).

The concept of truth itself becomes problematic within refugee status determination processes (cf. Daniel and Knudsen 1995; Fassin and d'Halluin 2005). Registration officers work with "UNHCR in-country information" gleaned from internet sources and internal documents, creating an official version of country conditions against which individual testimony is measured (Thomas 2006; Kagan 2003). This bureaucratic truth may not capture local variations, recent changes, or personal experiences that do not fit established patterns. The temporal dimensions of credibility assessment create additional challenges. Refugees may wait months or years between providing initial information and attending formal interviews, during which time their memories may fade, details may blur, or their understanding of what information is relevant may change (Cameron 2010). Life continues during these waiting periods, creating new experiences that may affect how refugees remember or narrate past events, experiences that inform their development of survival strategies in Malaysian society.

Some refugees engage in what might be termed strategic storytelling, adapting their narratives to meet perceived bureaucratic requirements rather than providing strictly accurate accounts of their experiences. This adaptation should be understood as a rational response to systems that demand particular types of evidence rather than simple deception. Research with asylum seekers in other contexts reveals how individuals learn which stories resonate with decision-makers and adapt their testimony accordingly. A female African asylum seeker in the United States, for example, constructed a narrative of rape by government soldiers not because this occurred, but because lawyers advised that sexual violence claims were more likely to succeed than other forms of persecution (Mehta 2011). Similar dynamics operate in Malaysia, where refugees share information about successful strategies, effective narratives, and the preferences of registration officers. This knowledge circulation enables some refugees to navigate the system more effectively while potentially disadvantaging those who lack access to community networks or who refuse to adapt their testimony. The emphasis on persecution narratives may also privilege certain types of suffering over others. Dramatic incidents of violence fit administrative categories more easily than gradual marginalization, economic discrimination, or social exclusion. Refugees who experienced systemic oppression rather than acute persecution may struggle to construct narratives that satisfy bureaucratic requirements, struggles that continue to affect how they present themselves in Malaysian society.

These individual struggles to navigate bureaucratic requirements took on new dimensions as the UNHCR shifted toward mass processing systems. The development of mass registration drives in Malaysia reflects both the UNHCR's attempts to manage overwhelming caseloads and the systematic nature of displacement from Myanmar. These large-scale operations, sometimes held in stadiums, attracted thousands of applicants from across the country and fundamentally changed the scale and nature of refugee status determination in Malaysia. Between 2008 and 2010, mass registration drives enabled the recognition of 75,000 refugees, representing a dramatic increase in Malaysia's officially recognized refugee population (Crisp, Obi and Umlas 2012). This expansion addressed humanitarian needs while creating new challenges for both the UNHCR and the Malaysian government, which viewed large refugee populations with increasing concern. The Cheras Stadium registration drive provides a revealing case study in how these operations functioned in practice. Originally designed for Rohingya registration, this event was overwhelmed when approximately 10,000 Chin refugees appeared, having learned about the drive through community networks and hoping to access registration opportunities previously denied to them.

The unexpected convergence of multiple ethnic groups at Cheras Stadium (Kuala Lumpur Stadium) exemplified a broader pattern of refugee agency within these mass-registration systems. The Chin refugee actions reflected both their desperation for recognition and their access to sophisticated information networks that enabled rapid mobilization across ethnic communities. Yet this determination to access registration opportunities came at considerable cost. The logistics of mass registration created new forms of vulnerability and exploitation. Refugees traveled across Kuala Lumpur and throughout peninsular Malaysia in response to rumors of upcoming registrations, often spending scarce resources on transportation while risking detection by authorities. These journeys represented significant investments for families with limited resources, further increasing the pressure to achieve successful registration outcomes. Mobile registration drives, conducted by UNHCR teams visiting regional cities and remote areas, addressed some access challenges while creating others. While these operations reduced travel costs and risks for refugees, they also operated with limited time and resources that affected the quality of status determination. Registration officers working under pressure with temporary facilities and interpreters could not provide the same careful review as available at the Kuala Lumpur compound.

The eruption of corruption scandals within UNHCR Malaysia's registration system further illuminated fundamental problems with refugee protection in a non-signatory state context (cf. Barnett and Finnemore 2004; Cooley and Ron 2002). For years, refugees reported systemic corruption within the registration team, including the availability of "fast-tracked" applications for cash payments and other forms of misconduct that undermined the integrity of status determination processes (Whitaker 2002). An Al Jazeera (2014) investigative report brought many of these allegations to public attention, forcing the UNHCR to acknowledge problems and implement reforms. The investigation revealed how corruption had become institutionalized within the registration system, affecting both individual cases and community confidence in protection mechanisms (cf. Rose-Ackerman 1999; Johnston 2005).

The allegations included claims that registration officers accepted bribes to expedite applications, manipulate interview outcomes, or provide favorable decisions to particular applicants (cf. Reno 1995; Szeftel 1998). These practices created a two-tiered system where wealthy refugees could purchase better treatment, while impoverished asylum seekers faced longer delays and less favorable consideration. The scandal also revealed problems with translator recruitment and oversight. Limited availability of qualified interpreters, combined with inadequate supervision, created opportunities for corruption and unprofessional behavior, thereby affecting the quality of status determination interviews. Refugee interpreters, often struggling financially themselves, faced temptations to accept payments for favorable interpretation or inside information about procedures. A Rohingya community leader directly confronted UNHCR leadership about institutional failures and corruption:

> I didn't get all information. I said, "You as the head, you sit down at the office. You do not know what's happening. You're not concerned what's happening outside. You really sit in the office. Your fieldwork staff know what's really happening to the refugees. You don't know. Now, all of you are responsible ... there's corruption committed by the staff." (Rohingya community leader, fieldwork interview, October 14, 2016)

The UNHCR's response included staff changes, procedural reforms, and enhanced oversight mechanisms designed to rebuild institutional credibility. New biometric identification cards were introduced to improve refugee documentation and reduce fraud, while training programs aimed to improve staff professionalism and ethical standards. However, trust in the UNHCR remained at historic lows among both refugee communities and the Malaysian government. Refugees questioned whether reforms addressed underlying problems or merely provided cosmetic improvements to discredited systems. Many continued to seek alternative pathways to protection, including fraudulent documentation and illegal border crossings to other countries. The Malaysian government used the corruption scandal to justify increased restrictions on refugee activities and enhanced screening of UNHCR operations. New identification requirements and registration procedures were thus aimed to appease political constituencies concerned about refugee numbers while providing Malaysian authorities with greater oversight of international humanitarian operations (Jalil and Hoffstaedter 2024).

BEYOND REGISTRATION: REFUGEE AGENCY IN LEGAL LIMBO

The achievement of formal refugee recognition through UNHCR registration represents both an end and a beginning for displaced persons in Malaysia. While status recognition provides crucial protection against deportation and enables access to limited services, it also establishes a foundation of precarity that shapes all subsequent experiences of life in Malaysia, as I explore throughout this book. Refugee status in Malaysia provides no legal rights under Malaysian domestic law, leaving protection entirely dependent on the UNHCR's continued presence and the Malaysian government's tolerance. This dependence creates ongoing anxiety for refugees who understand that their protection could disappear through policy changes, funding cuts, or political pressure. The legal limbo of refugee status means that recognized refugees cannot access formal employment, education, or social services available to Malaysian citizens or legal residents. While UNHCR registration provides some protection from arrest and deportation, it does not enable integration into Malaysian society or provide pathways to permanent settlement.

Economic survival, therefore, requires refugees to work in informal sectors where labor rights are minimal and exploitation is common. Without legal work authorization, refugees cannot demand fair wages, safe working conditions, or legal recourse when employers abuse them. This vulnerability creates cycles of poverty and dependence that affect entire families and communities. Educational access remains severely limited for refugee children, who cannot enroll in Malaysian government schools and depend on community-run education programs with minimal resources and recognition. This educational exclusion affects not only individual children but an entire generation's prospects for social mobility and integration. Healthcare access is episodic and expensive, as refugees often cannot access Malaysian public health services and must rely on private medical care, NGO clinics, or emergency treatment—often at a much higher cost to them. This limited access affects both individual health outcomes and community public health, creating vulnerabilities that extend beyond refugee populations.

The documentation provided through UNHCR registration—refugee cards and letters—provides some protection but remains vulnerable to loss, damage, or expiration. Refugees must carefully guard these documents as they navigate renewal processes that may involve months-long delays and uncertainty. Geographic mobility within Malaysia also remains constrained by immigration enforcement and police checkpoints, where refugees may face harassment, arrest, or extortion, regardless of their legal status with UNHCR. This limited mobility affects refugees' ability to access employment, services, or family connections across the country. The temporal dimensions of refugee status create additional challenges, as recognition provides no timeline for resolution through resettlement or return. Many refugees wait years or even decades in Malaysia without knowing whether their situations will improve, creating psychological stress and preventing long-term planning. Family unity remains precarious, since refugee status determination often occurs on an individual basis—as family members arrive at differing times or remain separated—and family members may receive different outcomes or processing timelines. Separation during flight, delayed arrival, or different legal statuses can divide families for years without a resolution mechanism in place.

Despite systemic challenges and legal constraints, refugees demonstrate remarkable creativity in navigating their path to recognition and building meaningful lives within Malaysia's protection gaps. These adaptive strategies show they retain agency and resilience built on the resourcefulness required for survival in legal limbo. Document acquisition and management have become crucial survival skills for refugees navigating multiple bureaucratic systems. Beyond UNHCR registration, refugees often seek documentation from community organizations, NGOs, and even commercial enterprises that can provide identification or access to services (Jalil and Hoffstaedter 2024). This portfolio approach to documentation reflects practical understanding that different documents serve different purposes and that redundancy provides security against loss or non-recognition. The value of documentation extends beyond official recognition to include psychological security and social status within refugee communities. Having papers—regardless of their legal significance—provides dignity and hope that resonates with cultural values about identity and belonging. For individuals who have been rendered stateless and documentation-less, any form of official recognition carries profound emotional significance.

Information networks within refugee communities develop sophisticated systems for sharing knowledge about registration processes, interview strategies, and bureaucratic requirements. These networks enable newer arrivals to benefit from collective community experience while creating informal mentorship relationships that provide social support beyond practical information. Storytelling and narrative preparation become community activities in which refugees help each other construct coherent, consistent testimonies that meet bureaucratic requirements while preserving essential truths about their persecution experiences. This collective narrative construction should be understood as an adaptation to system requirements rather than deception, representing rational responses to bureaucratic constraints. Economic strategies during the registration process often involve complex arrangements within refugee communities, including loans, labor exchanges, and resource sharing that enable individuals to survive while awaiting status determination.

Geographic strategies for refugees involve decisions about where to live, work, and access services, balancing cost, safety, community connections, and proximity to UNHCR facilities. Many refugees move frequently within Malaysia in response to employment opportunities, community conflicts, or changes in enforcement patterns that affect local security. Community organization membership often involves strategic choices about which groups to join, how actively to participate, and how to navigate internal politics that may affect individual registration prospects. Successful navigation requires understanding organizational dynamics, leadership preferences, and community expectations about proper behavior and loyalty. Meanwhile, some refugees acquire a level of legal literacy through informal education as they learn about their rights, bureaucratic procedures, and advocacy strategies. Asylum Access runs education and outreach programs that began during my fieldwork in 2015. This was a profound structural change in the availability of legal advice to refugees and in how the UNHCR handled appeals and challenges to its procedures. While few refugees possess any formal legal training, many develop a sophisticated understanding of protection systems and effective strategies for accessing available services or resolving problems.

Language acquisition and cultural adaptation occur simultaneously as refugees learn to navigate Malaysian society while maintaining connections to their homeland and diaspora. This bi- and often tri-cultural competence enables more effective interaction with Malaysian authorities, employers, and service providers while preserving important identity connections.

The process of becoming a refugee in Malaysia extends far beyond an administrative status change to encompass fundamental transformations in identity, social relationships, and life possibilities. This ontological shift occurs within a complex matrix of bureaucratic procedures, community networks, and individual adaptation strategies that create new forms of subjectivity while establishing precarious foundations for future life- and worldbuilding. The bureaucratic machinery of refugee status determination, centered on the UNHCR's registration processes, creates particular forms of subjectivity that emphasize documentation, consistency, and performance of victimhood as requirements for protection. Refugees must learn to present themselves in ways that satisfy these bureaucratic requirements while navigating language barriers, cultural differences, and trauma effects that complicate self-presentation. The physical and symbolic spaces of registration—the hilltop compound, the waiting cages, the air-conditioned interview rooms—create embodied experiences of hierarchy and dependence that shape the formation of refugee identity. These spatial arrangements communicate clear messages about who possesses agency and who must wait for decisions made by others.

Community organizations emerge as crucial intermediaries that both facilitate access to protection and create new forms of dependence and control (Riva and Hoffstaedter 2021). While these organizations provide essential services and advocacy, they also reproduce ethnic boundaries and hierarchies that may limit individual agency and social integration. The emphasis on ethnic identity verification in status determination processes requires refugees to perform authenticity in ways that may conflict with the fluid, contextual nature of identity itself. Language tests, cultural knowledge assessments, and community verification create bureaucratic truth about belonging that may not correspond to lived experience or self-understanding. Credibility assessment procedures further create tensions between bureaucratic requirements for consistent evidence and the complex realities of trauma, memory, and narrative construction. As outlined above, the demand for detailed, consistent testimony often conflicts with how human memory actually functions, particularly under conditions of persecution and displacement.

The need for mass registration drives demonstrates both the scale of displacement from Myanmar and the limitations of bureaucratic approaches to protection. While these operations enabled rapid status determination for thousands of refugees, they also created quality-control challenges and raised questions about the integrity of protection systems. Corruption scandals within UNHCR Malaysia revealed how protection systems designed to help refugees could become mechanisms for exploitation and abuse. The erosion of institutional trust affects not only individual cases but community confidence in protection mechanisms and international humanitarian institutions. The achievement of formal refugee status establishes a precarious foundation characterized by legal limbo, economic vulnerability, and dependence on international humanitarian assistance. While recognition provides crucial protection against, for example, deportation, it does not enable integration into Malaysian society or provide pathways to permanent settlement.

Refugee agency emerges through strategic adaptation and creative survival strategies that enable individuals and communities to navigate protection gaps while building meaningful lives despite systematic exclusion. These adaptive strategies demonstrate the resourcefulness and resilience that challenge victimization narratives while highlighting the creativity required for survival in difficult or hostile environments. The process of becoming a refugee in Malaysia ultimately exposes both the limitations of humanitarian protection systems and the remarkable resilience of displaced populations who must navigate these systems to access safety (cf. Betts and Collier 2017; Zetter 2007). Understanding this process requires attention not only to formal bureaucratic procedures but to the complex social, cultural, and existential dimensions of identity transformation that occur within protection gaps (Long 2013; Fiddian-Qasmiyeh et al. 2014).

This analysis suggests the need for protection approaches that recognize refugee agency while addressing structural constraints that create vulnerability and dependence (cf. Jacobsen 2005; Crisp 2004). Rather than focusing solely on status determination procedures, effective protection requires attention to the broader social, economic, and political contexts that shape refugee experiences and opportunities for dignity and self-determination (Zetter 2014; Bakewell 2008). The Malaysian case demonstrates how non-signatory states create specific challenges for refugee protection while also revealing innovative adaptation strategies developed by both refugees and humanitarian actors. These experiences provide important insights into displacement and protection in contexts where formal legal frameworks provide minimal security or recognition. Ultimately, the process of becoming a refugee represents a profound transformation that affects not only legal status but fundamental aspects of identity, belonging, and life possibilities. Understanding this transformation requires analytical frameworks that capture both the constraints imposed by protection systems and the agency exercised by refugees who must navigate these systems to access safety and build meaningful lives in exile, lives that I explore in detail throughout the subsequent chapters of this book.

CHAPTER 4

Place-making in the Polycrisis

Refugee Agency and Resilience

REFRAMING CRISIS: FROM EMERGENCY TO POLYCRISIS

The dictionary definition of a crisis is a "decisive point" or a moment in time when a crucial decision must be made, for better or worse—but even not making a decision will be a decision of sorts—and its Latin origins point to the moment of truth when a disease was either overcome and a person would get better, or die. A crisis is thus a true limit concept that brings to the fore the decisive moment in time and space in which some kind of action is required, or, where even inaction has consequences. Jaspers (1967) called the limit concept a *Grenzsituation*, literally a border situation in which our existential framing is shattered, and we are able to see through the vast mist of the everyday and our mundane existence through to the transcendental. Jaspers saw death as the ultimate *limit situation*, or at least as one's realization of our finitude. In my work with refugees in Southeast Asia, the legal limbo refugees live within places them in an ongoing limit situation; the pervasive manner in which policymakers and service providers alike discuss refugees is in terms of an imminent crisis. This is especially true for a transit country like Malaysia that is central to the unfolding refugee "crisis" in Southeast Asia. Rather than accepting this framing uncritically, I want to address this characterization of the "refugee" and the broader refugee issue in the region, building on the daily experiences of exclusion and survival of refugees there.

Regional states and the international community often frame large population movements as a crisis to conjure up notions of disorder. This leads to the securitization of mobility in the region. ASEAN, national governments, and civil society have rarely addressed regional refugee movements in a concerted effort and have relied either on internationally led interventions, such as the Comprehensive Plan of Action for Indo-Chinese Refugees, or ad hoc local approaches like the ones we have seen in parts of Malaysia (such as for Moro refugees in Sabah). This approach demands we ask: for whom is it a crisis (see Roitman 2021, 2)? Often, when an influx of refugee boats on the shore triggers a state to declare a unidimensional crisis, the announcement hides the structural and underlying causes of such displacements. Transit and destination countries, such as Malaysia, also deepen the crisis by not acknowledging refugees, retaining them in legal limbo, and then continually engaging in othering processes to subdue, dehumanize, and marginalize them. But is this actually a crisis? The question requires both empirical examination and theoretical unpacking. The raw numbers seem to suggest ever more people are being displaced and becoming refugees. According to recent UN figures, there are now over 117 million people displaced worldwide and about 42 million refugees, i.e., people who have fled across borders (UNHCR 2026a). Large numbers to be sure, but as sociologist Hein de Haas (2008, 2023) has argued, the numbers tell a particular kind of story: a crisis story that helps the aid sector procure funds. Yet when we examine these figures more carefully, a different picture emerges. The official figures indicate that there are about 28.5 million refugees under UNHCR's mandate (UNHCR 2026b). This figure rises to about 34.5 million if we include Palestinian refugees, who are under UNRWA's (United Nations Relief and Works Agency for Palestine Refugees in the Near East) mandate (UNHCR 2026b). This means about 0.4 percent of the total world population (roughly 8.3 billion people) are currently refugees (UN DESA 2024).

Another way to view the numbers for a more realistic version of the refugee "crisis story" is to look at the number of international migrants moving around worldwide. This number has remained remarkably stable since the 1960s at roughly 3 percent of the world population. According to 2017 UN figures, there were 260 million international migrants; that means refugees only make up about 10 percent of that number. Refugee numbers fluctuate more significantly, driven by varying conflict levels in origin regions and by push-and-pull factors that determine whether people can leave and where they can find refuge. So, the numbers vary, but over the long term, trends suggest the *true* crisis is that we continue along the same path with the same policies and restrictions that endanger more and more people. And it must be said that all the heavy lifting in a crisis situation is usually done by countries in the global South, which predominantly host refugees, look after them, permit refugee camps and cities to emerge, and sometimes allow refugees to work. Such a complex and fragmented legal, policy, and sociopolitical environment evokes the recently adopted and adapted notion of the polycrisis, which denotes the multiplicity and cascading effects of multiple crises (Tooze 2022). Polycrisis speaks to the "complex intersolidarity of problems, antagonisms, [and] crises" (Morin and Kern 1999, 74) of the current displacements in Southeast Asia and their effects on domestic and regional policy. This polycrisis becomes evident when examining Malaysia's contradictory position in the regional refugee landscape. When we speak about protection regimes in Southeast Asia and Oceania, there are few countries that are signatories to the Refugee Convention and Protocol, and even fewer that take this responsibility seriously by providing sanctuary and protection to refugees who turn up at their borders. Malaysia is not a signatory and has a very poor record of treating many of its foreign workers. And here is a major issue where protection and work, the moral and legal obligations, collide with the economy: Malaysia would not be as prosperous as it is without millions of foreign workers laboring, building skyscrapers like the Petronas Twin Towers, manufacturing semiconductors, and cleaning the streets. Refugees make up a small percentage of those workers, but a crucial one, as refugees have to work to survive. The UNHCR has limited funding, and in Malaysia, it mainly registers refugees, so that only a precious few can be resettled. However, it has no money to provide refugee services, so refugees must fend for themselves. This means refugees must earn enough money to pay for healthcare, refugee community schools for their children, remit to their families, and on the list goes.

The opportunity this affords many refugees is the chance to escape extreme poverty. In 2019, I spent some time in Myanmar's Chin State, the country's poorest state with the least infrastructure. And though the political situation at that point was relatively stable, the economic deprivation from decades of fighting, effective military occupation, and no investment was evident. As a result, few Chin returned to Chin State during the brief interlude between military rule. Indeed, people continued to leave because they were so poor and without hope that the future would bring better conditions for them there. This is how we must understand the complex interplay of push-and-pull factors that drive refugee movements—systemic economic factors are often a part of the reason for such mixed, complex movements. This is the reality that the state-centric crisis narratives systematically obscure. To understand the complexity of push-and-pull factors that demonstrate the role this larger global system of capitalism, identity, and religion can play in refugee movements, I also want to draw attention to the situation in Rakhine State, Myanmar, where I spent time in 2019. Myanmar has systematically excluded the Rohingya from its body politic, depriving them of their citizenship, persecuting them, and killing them. Rohingya have been internally displaced to live in refugee camps, which are effectively ghettos in and around towns they used to call home. Many have fled overseas, many have been trafficked, and it is here that crossing borders really becomes a crisis. Let me illustrate this with the story of Ahmad, a Rohingya refugee who arrived in Malaysia in 2017. Like many Rohingya, he had been detained in a camp for internally displaced people close to the beach near Rakhine's capital, Sittwe. The authorities often leave the camps open to the sea to allow for some fishing and for Rohingya to be smuggled and trafficked on boats down the coast to Bangladesh, down to Yangon, and then onwards to China, Thailand, and Malaysia. Many Rohingya are desperate to leave, so they will jump aboard passing boats whether they know the destination or not. Ahmad had asked around and thought he secured a "good" boat—more expensive but less likely to be a front for trafficking, for example, one where he might be sold into slavery on a fishing boat in Thailand. So, Ahmad pawned his belongings and paid smugglers to take him to Malaysia.

Why Malaysia? Many Rohingya already live there, as Rohingya have been fleeing Myanmar for decades; Malaysia is also seen as a Muslim country that will (or at least should) provide sanctuary for fellow Muslim refugees, like the Rohingya; and finally, Rohingya know that they will be able to work there and earn "good money," or at least much more than in Myanmar, where they are heavily restricted in what they can do. Ahmad waited for the boat, and when he got word, he went out to the beach and boarded a small fishing vessel already filled with people. He was told they would rendezvous with a larger vessel in the open water and then continue on a month-long journey to Malaysia. But that was a lie. Ahmad's journey was cut short in Thailand. The boat landed, and upon disembarking, he was beaten and tied up in a trafficking camp. This has become a common story of deception and extortion. Many Rohingya end up in such trafficking camps along the Thai-Malaysian border, where they are ransomed by the traffickers. Ahmad's family and friends in Malaysia had to pay a ransom to free him. Much of this is documented and could not happen without the tacit approval of authorities on both sides of the border (Hoffstaedter and Missbach 2021). Thailand has prosecuted and imprisoned some police and immigration officials, whereas Malaysia has only investigated some and has not pursued any charges.

Once Ahmad arrived in Malaysia, he was in debt to family members and had to begin working immediately to pay it off. He found work as a grass cutter, working all day along the federal motorway in and around Kuala Lumpur. Refugees, like Ahmad, are integral to the low-wage segment of Malaysia's economy: staffing kitchens, collecting scrap, working on palm oil plantations, assembling semiconductors, and growing vegetables in the Cameron Highlands. Thus, they provide cheap labor for dirty, dangerous, and demeaning jobs. They do this because it is necessary for their survival, but the relationship is not one-sided: Malaysia's economy actively depends on this reservoir of cheap, undocumented labor to fill roles at pay rates that documented workers will not accept. It is precisely this structural demand that has made Malaysia a sought-after place of first asylum: refugees come because the work is there, and it is usually better paid than what they could achieve in their home country or other places of refuge (see Jalil 2023).

FIGURE 6 Refugee scrap collectors working in Kuala Lumpur's informal economy

FROM CAMPS TO CITIES: THEORIZING URBAN REFUGEE PLACE-MAKING

Ahmad's story of debt, labor, and survival in Malaysia's informal economy illustrates a broader transformation in refugee experiences. While refugees like Ahmad carve out precarious existences in urban labor markets by becoming indispensable yet invisible parts of metropolitan economies, scholars have only recently begun to theorize these urban refugee realities beyond the camp paradigm. For a long time, theorizing refugees meant theorizing the camp, encampment, and enclosures as spaces for and of refugees. The camp was seen as the archetypal refugee space, with Giorgio Agamben's (1998) concept of the "state of exception" profoundly shaping the discourse. Agamben theorized refugee camps as paradigmatic spaces where sovereign power suspends normal juridical order, reducing inhabitants to "bare life" or mere biological existence stripped of political rights and citizenship. Michel Agier's (2002; 2011) ethnographic work complemented and complicated this framework by examining camps as liminal spaces of exclusion that nonetheless generate new forms of social life and political subjectivity. This camp-centric scholarship, alongside work by scholars like Liisa Malkki (1995a, 1995b) on refugees in and around camps in Africa and Barbara Harrell-Bond's (1986) critiques of dependency, established camps as both the empirical and conceptual center of refugee studies. However, today, more than half of all refugees reside in urban settings; they face different spatial environments, navigate different, often longer and more complex routes to safety, and contend with new challenges along the way. This shift from camps to cities fundamentally alters the dynamics of refugee place-making. Appadurai's theory of "locality production" provides crucial insights for making a better sense of these urban dynamics. However, this framework requires adaptation when applied to refugee experiences under polycrisis conditions. Drawing on Appadurai's theory of "locality production," we can see how refugee settlements in Malaysia operate simultaneously as context-produced and context-generative spaces. Refugees remain "increasingly prisoners in the context-producing activities of the nation-state, which makes their own efforts to produce locality seem feeble, even doomed" (Appadurai 1996, 186); nonetheless, they find ways to generate new contexts within these constraints. Understanding the processes through which people experience place and their emplacement becomes bound up with their social and personal identity, requires treating place not as a two-dimensional setting in which the social world eventuates, but as a product of the social world emerging itself.

The social worlds that refugees construct involve active engagement with their lost homelands. Elizabeth Colson's (1971, 49ff.) pioneering research showed how Gwembe villagers, forced from their homes by Zambia's Kariba Dam, inscribed their new settlements with the names of former neighborhoods, effectively overlaying present spaces with memories of the past. What emerges from this scholarship is a repertoire of place-making practices that refugees deploy across contexts to anchor themselves: narrating accounts of life before displacement, reconstructing elements of familiar landscapes, carrying treasured objects, and preserving ties to people and places left behind (Dudley 2010). As Malkki (1995a) demonstrates in her ethnography of

Burundian refugees, these practices work to sustain connections across spatial and temporal ruptures through narrative and memory. These are not passive acts of nostalgia but active efforts to bridge the ruptures created by displacement.

Building on these insights while recognizing the specific challenges of the polycrisis environment, recent scholarship has emphasized refugee agency in urban contexts. As Sigona (2012, 51) argues,

> attentiveness to the role of exogenous factors in shaping the condition of "illegality" should not construct undocumented migrants as passive and agency-less subjects overdetermined by structural conditions, or undocumentedness as a homogeneous and undifferentiated experience.

He further notes that undocumented migrants "are resilient and resourceful, and display significant capacity to adapt to the situation in the country of residence" (51). This adaptive capacity becomes particularly evident in the strategies refugees develop for navigating Malaysia's complex legal and economic landscape.

BUILDING ALTERNATIVE (AGRICULTURAL) WORLDS

These theoretical insights become concrete when examining refugee farming communities outside Kuala Lumpur (see chapter 6). The agricultural dimension of refugee place-making provides particularly clear examples of how polycrisis navigation operates in practice. In 2012, I spent most of three months living on a farm in Batu Arang, about 50km from Kuala Lumpur. It was designated as the Chin farm, as it was set up by a Chin refugee organization, with a refugee couple, Simon and his wife Mary, running it. Their farm had only been established three months prior to my arrival. At this time in Rakhine State, Myanmar, Rohingya and Rakhine were violently clashing, which led to the deaths and displacement of thousands, predominantly Rohingya. Neighboring Simon and Mary's farm had been another run by Rakhine, but they became frightened of the Rohingya living in the area and were warned that they may be targeted for reprisals. They had fled just a week before my arrival, leaving Simon in charge of their farm, chickens, and dogs. This illustrates how conflict in their homeland and the associated terror and fear can follow refugees into exile, leaving them vulnerable and anxious (O'Brien and Hoffstaedter 2020).

Despite these challenges, refugee farming communities demonstrate remarkable place-making innovations. This community was made up of several farms run by Chin and Karen organizations, but occupied by families who looked after the farms and operated them as businesses. The family structure and support network that came with this built up resilience, coping mechanisms, and a sense of belonging to a group of people with whom they share deep connections (of language, ethnicity, and/or culture). The family unit operates as such a space, which anchors refugees. On a Sunday, I joined a group from the Karen farm on a foraging trip, something that all refugees living in this community do to survive and supplement their incomes and diets. We all drove scooters to one of the lakes that dotted the landscape, which were, in fact, old open mines filled with water. Once there, we descended to the water's edge with each of us holding an empty basket. We were to fill it with mussels submerged along the muddy water's edge. Within minutes, we had found ten, and after moving along the shoreline, sometimes feeling for them with our feet or diving for them in deeper water, we filled the baskets to the brim. The harvesting required intimate ecological knowledge: where mussels clustered, how to distinguish them by touch underwater, and which sizes indicated good eating. This knowledge circulated within the farm community through apprenticeship-style learning, with experienced foragers teaching newcomers the locations and techniques that maximized harvest while minimizing risk. The practice connected refugees to the Malaysian landscape in ways that transcended their legal exclusion, enabling them to extract sustenance from environments that formally denied them belonging. We returned to the Karen farm for a shared meal, with everyone present on the farm sharing food, stories, and presence, just being together. The mussels were quickly steamed with ginger and lemongrass, their briny flavor providing welcome protein for people subsisting primarily on rice and vegetables. The meal's nutritional value proved less significant than its social function. Just being together, as opposed to being isolated and alone in urban apartments, provided therapeutic effects. The communal gathering created space for storytelling, for processing daily events, for maintaining a connection with Myanmar through shared memories, while building new bonds in Malaysia.

Meanwhile, on the Chin farm next door, a new family was growing into itself. Simon and Mary were working hard to build up a farm from scratch, as well as to create a network of friends who regularly came to the farm to "just be there" and spend time together (hoping, as one refugee remarked, that Simon had again been successful at hunting for wild boar and would be sharing the food). One evening, two of Simon's refugee friends came over for one such informal chitchat. As the muezzin's call to prayer wafted across the humid evening air, this group of refugees sitting together, drinking instant coffee and chatting about the day's events, was utterly oblivious to the wider world acting upon them, their precarity, or the liminality of their lives. As we chatted about a monkey that had been ensnared in one of Simon's wild boar traps and life in Batu Arang in general, a sense of community and shared concern was evident.

FIGURE 7 Foraging for mussels in lakes formed by abandoned mines near Batu Arang to supplement farm income

Yet this scene of domestic tranquility on Simon's farm represented only one dimension of refugee farming life. The broader community dynamics across neighboring farms revealed patterns of mutual support, intergenerational care, and resourcefulness that extended well beyond individual households. While I was staying in Batu Arang, two young Chin women had moved into the neighboring Karen farm, newly arrived in Malaysia with no employment and nowhere else to go. The Karen refugee organization temporarily placed them on the farm while they searched for jobs in the city, transforming the agricultural site into a transit point and orientation space for new arrivals.

The young women's integration into farm life illuminated how these spaces functioned as cultural incubators. They helped the grandmother make chili powder, all three sitting together, talking and working in unison as they separated the chili from the stalks. The girls were respectful of the woman, whom they called "grandmother" despite no blood relation, and she, in turn, mothered them, showing them how to do things more efficiently, chatting about life in Malaysia, and genuinely caring about what their lives would be like from now on. This intergenerational knowledge transfer from elders to youth, from experienced refugees to newcomers, created fictive kinship bonds while transmitting practical skills and cultural knowledge that would prove essential for urban survival.

As evening fell across the farms, the different temporal rhythms compared to urban refugee life became evident. In Kuala Lumpur, refugees moved through time with constant vigilance, scanning for threats, calculating risks with each journey outside their homes. On the farms, time stretched differently. While working hours were long, usually all sunlight hours daily with only one day off monthly, within that structure existed moments of relative peace: the morning's first coffee while surveying growing plants, the afternoon break in the shade, the evening gathering after work was concluded. These temporal rhythms echoed the rhythms of agricultural life in Myanmar, providing psychological continuity even as specific crops and landscapes varied.

The social interactions further demonstrated the farms' role as sites of cross-cultural encounter that challenged Malaysia's ethnic hierarchies. Leaving the farm one day, we passed a group of motorbikes parked roadside. In the distance, men were playing football on a makeshift field. "Orang Asli and Chin playing together," my host explained. "They have become friends here." This simple observation revealed a profound possibility that shared marginality could generate unexpected transversal solidarities, that indigenous Malaysians and refugees might find common ground through sport and proximity, that the farms created spaces where national and ethnic boundaries temporarily dissolved through everyday interaction.

FIGURE 8 Processing chilies on the Karen refugee farm near Batu Arang: intergenerational knowledge transfer and fictive kinship building

It was just another evening at a farmhouse with friends chatting away about the day's work and their lives. The seemingly banal normality of it made it all the more significant. This sort of place- and world-making that refugee farmers engage in is hard work and requires not just the physical construction of dwellings and gardens, but also the social aspects of ritual, community, and neighborliness (Appadurai 1996, 179ff.; Turton 2005).

The contrast between city life and life on the farm could not be starker. In the city, refugees have to be constantly attentive, scanning and aware of the state scanning for them (police, immigration officers, etc.). On the farm, they feel less exhausted from the constant fear of detection and anxiety about others.

HEALTH AND SURVIVAL IN THE POLYCRISIS

The health system provides another example of how polycrisis dynamics shape refugee place-making strategies. When I lived on the refugee-run farm with Simon and his wife, Mary was expecting her first baby; although she was experiencing problems, she was too scared to go to the hospital. I spoke to her husband about this, and Simon explained that they had heard many stories of families being arrested in the hospital and detained in immigration detention camps with newborn babies. Second, they could not afford the treatment fees, which in Malaysia are considerably higher for foreigners. Third, because of their relatively remote location, transport was costly; there was no public transport to the hospital, and a taxi fare was beyond their means. For refugees, this means that many diseases and health issues are not attended to or are deferred until they become life-threatening. In another case, Simon's cousin's wife was having a difficult pregnancy, and a refugee health organization referred them to a major Kuala Lumpur hospital. However, they were denied treatment there, as they did not have a UNHCR card or passport. Increasingly, Malaysian hospitals have become places of fear and surveillance, rather than places of sanctuary and care.

These local struggles with healthcare, work, and survival must be understood within larger global patterns of mobility and immobility. It is important to note that the ability to cross borders, to seek better opportunities, and to escape persecution—in short, movement writ large—remains a privilege for relatively few. People move, and often they move for mixed reasons, including poverty. According to novelist Mohsin Hamid (*The Reluctant Fundamentalist, Exit West*), the political deadlock on migration in America and Europe reflects a collective refusal to accept the reality of mass population movements. Hamid said,

> The more that people who are economically freezing and precarious become aware of places where people are economically warmer and more safe, the more they want to move.... We need to figure out how to build a vision for this coming reality that isn't a disaster, that is humane and even inspiring. (Freeman 2016)

This insight captures the fundamental challenge facing policymakers and host societies: how to develop responses to human mobility that acknowledge both its inevitability and its potential benefits, rather than treating it as a crisis to be managed through securitization and exclusion. These examples show how place-making in a polycrisis requires refugees to develop sophisticated strategies that work across multiple domains of constraint and opportunity simultaneously. Rather than simply responding to isolated crises, refugees create integrated approaches to survival and belonging that address legal, economic, health, and social challenges as interconnected elements of their lived experience. Their place-making practices create spaces of belonging and security within often hostile environments, while simultaneously unsettling dominant ideas about Malaysian national identity through their very existence.

The polycrisis framework allows us to understand refugee experiences not as exceptional or temporary disruptions to an otherwise stable order, but as ongoing navigations of structural intersecting vulnerabilities that characterize contemporary global capitalism and the global order. In this light, refugee place-making becomes not just a survival strategy but a form of world-making that offers insights into alternative ways of organizing social and economic life. Through their daily practices of creating home, community, and belonging under conditions of legal exclusion and economic marginalization, refugees demonstrate forms of resilience and innovation that challenge dominant assumptions about citizenship, belonging, and the nation-state itself.

The following chapters will explore specific dimensions of this place-making process, examining how refugees navigate the city (chapter 5), create economic opportunities through farming (chapter 6), and build community through sport and cultural celebration (chapter 7). Together, these chapters depict the full complexity of refugee agency within Malaysia's shrinking protection environment, showing how survival and thriving can coexist within structures of exclusion and marginalization, and how refugees develop innovative strategies transcending simple adaptation to create new forms of social organization and belonging that challenge dominant assumptions about citizenship, belonging, and the possibilities for more inclusive forms of political community.

CHAPTER 5

"Being" a Refugee in Urban Kuala Lumpur

On a Tuesday morning in Ampang, I watch refugees navigate a city's neighborhood with practiced precision. At the corner shop, a Chin man serves tea to Malaysian office workers who barely glance at him. Across the road, Rohingya workers cut the grass along the busy main road, their movements efficient and unobtrusive. Two blocks down, a group of refugees pauses at an intersection, scanning for police before crossing. They inhabit Kuala Lumpur's streets, work in its businesses, rent its apartments, but they move through the city as if they do not quite exist. Their Malaysian neighbors seem to participate in this same fiction, acknowledging refugees only in the specific roles they perform: waiter, cleaner, mechanic, gardener. Two populations occupy the same urban space through an elaborate practice of mutual unseeing.

INTRODUCTION: UNSEEING AND THE TOPOLGANGER IN THE CITY

Understanding how refugees create lives in Kuala Lumpur requires examining the spatial logic of urban coexistence under conditions of legal exclusion. Nation-states assert sovereignty through what might be called domestication or the confluence of domination and home-building. Malaysia attempts to reign supreme over citizens and non-citizens within its claimed boundaries, distributing access to an emotional register of homeliness to those it recognizes as "its" people. As a non-signatory to the UN Refugee Convention, Malaysia makes no distinction between refugees and undocumented migrants, leaving both groups in legal limbo. This judicial uncertainty unsettles the *a priori* status of the nation itself, and the refugee becomes "nothing less than a limit concept that radically calls into question the fundamental categories of the nation state" (Agamben 1998, 78).

Yet refugees are more than limit concepts. Dunn and Cons (2013) demonstrate in their work on internally displaced camps that Agamben's notion of bare life proves a dead end for understanding real people anthropologically, limiting both agency and the discovery of otherness. They argue instead for "aleatory sovereignty," or literally, rule by contingency, replacing Agamben's monolithic sovereign power with recognition of how sovereignty's iterative enactment makes it "fragile, unpredictable and haphazard" (3). In Malaysia, as in camps, multiple authorities act upon refugees, seeking to contain them, while refugees find ways of resisting and engaging in alternative politics in spaces that might be termed outside-domestication.

Humphrey (2004, 421) describes an inside-outside form of sovereignty where "sovereignty itself, which has to consist of practices, may be rethought not simply as a set of political capacities but as a formation in society that engages with ways of life that have temporality and their own characteristic aesthetics." Refugees engage in diverse practices to reclaim agency over their lives, yet space appears immutable and state-sanctioned, ostensibly beyond their control. As Isin (2002, 49) notes, space functions as "a fundamental strategic property by which groups, nations, societies, federations, empires and kingdoms are constituted in the real world, and through this constitution, structured as 'objective' realities." Outside-domestication suggests spaces and modalities of being that escape the instrumental logic of modernity and its greatest champion, the nation-state. These spaces either generate their own logics or duplicate alternative modalities within spaces shared with the domesticated.

How can we conceptualize two realities occupying shared space? Elizabeth Dunn (2017) deploys China Miéville's fictitious "topolganger," which fuses "topography" and "doppelganger," to make sense of the multiplicity of spaces and how they are used and perceived in refugee camps. In Miéville's (2009) novel *The City & the City*, two cities occupy identical physical space, each manifested by "unseeing" the other. This strategy pervades the refugee experience: host societies pretend refugees are not there, while refugees try to "fly under the radar" to avoid detection. Two or more communities live side by side without interacting with the other as "other."

In central Kuala Lumpur, Malaysians largely ignore the sizeable refugee presence that serves them coffee, repairs their cars, or builds their homes and offices. These workers remain invisible to middle and upper-class citizens who see them simply as "foreign workers." Chin refugees particularly reimagine their homeland in Malaysia according to ethno-linguistic and spatial belonging. They register with their refugee organization based on specific ethno-linguistic representations: Kachin, Karen, or Chin. The Chin further subdivide themselves into organizations based on their townships of origin, like Hakha and Falam. Entry requires proving belonging through language or kinship connections. This re-emplacement creates a topolganger situation in which Chin refugees dwell simultaneously in Malaysia and in their respective hometowns by association.

Mobilities depend fundamentally on access to money, class, social, and cultural capital. Invisibility functions both as a protective shield and an economic strategy. The practice of unseeing operates by both Malaysians and refugees navigating an ostensibly shared urban space. However, when these parallel worlds collide, breaches occur. COVID-19 created such a breach when authorities suddenly identified a large population of undocumented people as potential disease vectors (Munro and Hoffstaedter 2020), exposing the fragility of refuge created outside modes of domestication. This breach revealed what daily life in Kuala Lumpur normally obscures through mutual unseeing: the ongoing ontic insecurity that structures refugee existence in the city.

This topolganger logic of urban coexistence creates what Kinnvall (2004) and Richmond (1994) identify as ontic insecurity, i.e., the fundamental uncertainty about one's very existence and place in the world that extends beyond immediate physical safety to encompass questions of legal status, economic viability, and social recognition. Here, Malkki's (1995a) insight that displacement and emplacement constitute inverse processes offers particular purchase for understanding refugee urban experience. Rather than viewing displacement as the absence of place, this framework suggests that refugees engage in ongoing processes of emplacement that create new forms of belonging and attachment within host cities. However, refugee emplacement in Kuala Lumpur occurs within conditions of severe ontic insecurity that pervades every aspect of daily life, from interactions with authorities to accessing basic services, yet paradoxically also creates conditions for innovative adaptation and community formation.

NAVIGATING THE CITY: BEYOND SURVEILLANCE AND TOWARD MUTUALITY

The daily reality of refugee life in Kuala Lumpur is shaped by the constant possibility of arrest, detention, and deportation that accompanies legal exclusion from Malaysian society. These encounters represent breaches in the topolganger logic described above, i.e., moments when mutual unseeing breaks down and refugees become hypervisible to state authorities. This legal precarity manifests most acutely in encounters with police and immigration authorities, which demonstrate both the arbitrary nature of law enforcement and the sophisticated survival strategies refugees develop to navigate official hostility. As one refugee community organizer explained when discussing strategies for securing the release of detained refugees, the outcomes of police encounters follow depressingly predictable patterns: approximately 10 percent of detained refugees can be released simply through advocacy and discussion with police officers; about 30 percent are formally charged and end up in immigration detention where only UNHCR intervention can secure their release; while the majority, 60 percent, are released upon payment of bribes to the arresting officers. This demonstrates the prevalence of corruption within Malaysia's police and immigration enforcement system and, moreover, the ways in which refugee vulnerability becomes a source of profit for state agents.

The 10 percent of cases resolved through dialogue represent moments when police officers exercise discretion in favor of refugees, often influenced by factors such as the perceived legitimacy of refugee claims, the intervention of respected community leaders, or simple human compassion. These encounters show that even within systems of exclusion, individual agency and relationship-building can create spaces for mercy and recognition. Community organizers work to cultivate relationships with local police through educating officers about refugee status and building social capital that can be mobilized during enforcement operations. However, the 30 percent of refugees who face formal charges and detention represent the full force of Malaysia's exclusionary legal framework. Immigration detention centers become spaces where refugees experience the most acute forms of state violence, separated from families and communities while awaiting deportation back to countries from which they fled for protection. The fact that only UNHCR intervention can secure release from detention means both the complete exclusion of refugees from Malaysian legal protections and their total dependence on international humanitarian actors for basic rights.

Most significantly, the 60 percent of cases resolved through bribery expose systemic corruption. The expectation of bribes creates a form of informal taxation on the refugee presence in Malaysia, requiring communities to maintain funds for securing releases while normalizing extortion as a condition of urban survival. This corruption simultaneously undermines the rule of law while creating predictable costs that refugees can plan for and manage through community cooperation. One Rohingya refugee described the routine nature of police harassment despite having legal documentation:

> When I showed them my UNHCR card, they still checked my wallet. They found money but didn't take it. I don't know why they're checking the wallet.... They are very rude. Not very rude, this is medium. Sometimes they're angry. (Rohingya interlocutor, fieldwork interview, September 9, 2016)

Another Rohingya refugee recounted a more confrontational encounter in which he refused to pay bribes:

> The police officer stopped me and asked me about the document. When I don't have it, they try to take money from me. They just simply threaten me that they are going to arrest me, put me in jail. I say "Ok. If you want to arrest me without committing any crime, ok you can arrest me. I don't have money for you." (Rohingya interlocutor, fieldwork interview, October 2, 2016)

Negotiating police encounters requires refugees to develop sophisticated skills in reading official attitudes, managing documentation, and presenting themselves in ways that minimize arrest risk. Many refugees carry multiple forms of identification, such as UNHCR cards, community organization membership cards, and work permits from previous employers, hoping that one document might provide protection during police encounters. The effectiveness of these documents depends entirely on the knowledge and disposition of individual officers, creating uncertainty that requires constant vigilance and adaptation. Thus, refugees must learn to navigate a range of uncertainties to survive and literally move forward (cf. Vigh 2009). Spatial strategies also prove crucial for avoiding police encounters. Refugees develop detailed knowledge of enforcement patterns, learning which areas face regular raids, which times of day present greater risk, and which routes provide safer passage through the city. This knowledge circulates through community networks, enabling refugees to adjust their movements and activities in response to current enforcement priorities. Markets, construction sites, and residential areas with high refugee concentrations become sites of heightened surveillance that require careful navigation. The psychological impact of the constant arrest risk cannot be overstated. Many refugees describe living in permanent anxiety, always alert to the presence of police and ready to flee or hide when necessary. This hypervigilance affects sleep patterns, social relationships, and mental health, creating forms of trauma that extend far beyond the original persecution that forced their displacement in the first place. Children growing up in refugee families often internalize these fears, learning to view uniformed authority as threatening rather than protective.

Access to healthcare in Malaysia reveals perhaps most starkly the human costs of refugee legal exclusion, while simultaneously demonstrating the complex survival strategies that displaced communities develop to address basic needs. Malaysian hospitals, rather than serving as spaces of sanctuary and care, have increasingly become sites of surveillance and exclusion where refugees face arrest, deportation, and financial exploitation alongside medical emergencies. The experience of Mary recounted above, a pregnant refugee woman living on a farm outside Kuala Lumpur, illustrates the multiple barriers that prevent refugees from accessing essential healthcare services. Despite experiencing complications during her first pregnancy, she remained too frightened to seek hospital treatment due to widespread reports of families being arrested in medical facilities and detained in immigration centers with their newborn babies. The transformation of hospitals from spaces of healing into sites of state surveillance exemplifies how breaches in the topolganger logic can occur anywhere, making even seeking medical care a calculated risk.

Beyond arrest fears, economic barriers create additional obstacles to healthcare access. Medical treatment costs for foreigners in Malaysia are considerably higher than for citizens, placing even basic care beyond the reach of most refugee families. Emergency services, specialist consultations, and surgical procedures require immediate cash payments that can consume months of wages for families already struggling to survive. These cost differentials create a two-tiered healthcare system where citizenship status directly determines access to treatment. A Rohingya refugee explained the prohibitive cost of healthcare access: "Registration costs RM 100 at government hospital. Because if local people pay RM 1, foreigners pay RM 100. Every time we go, we need registration. Registration itself costs RM 100" (Rohingya interlocutor, fieldwork interview, October 27, 2016). Transportation costs add another layer of exclusion, particularly for refugees living in rural or peri-urban areas where public transport remains limited or non-existent. The pregnant woman's remote location meant that even reaching a hospital required expensive taxi fares that exceeded the family's income. This geographic isolation compounds legal exclusion, creating spaces where refugees remain invisible to both state services and potential humanitarian assistance.

The temporal dimensions of healthcare exclusion prove particularly devastating for refugees experiencing medical emergencies. Many delay treatment until conditions become life-threatening, hoping that symptoms will resolve themselves without professional intervention, or with minimal herbal or traditional remedies. This deferral strategy, while economically rational, often results in more serious health complications that require expensive emergency treatment. The lack of preventive care and regular check-ups creates cycles of health crises that can drain family resources while perpetuating medical vulnerability. Documentation requirements add administrative barriers that can prove insurmountable for refugees seeking medical care. The case of a refugee woman denied treatment at a major Kuala Lumpur hospital because she lacked a UNHCR card or passport demonstrates how bureaucratic requirements exclude even those facing serious medical emergencies. Hospital staff, uncertain about refugee status and concerned about payment guarantees, often refuse treatment rather than risk institutional liability.

These exclusions from formal healthcare systems force refugees to develop alternative medical networks that combine traditional healing practices, informal practitioners, and emergency-only engagement with Malaysian hospitals. Community healers, often refugees themselves, can provide basic medical care using knowledge from homeland practices adapted to Malaysian contexts. Traditional medicines, herbal remedies, and spiritual healing practices fill some gaps left by formal medical exclusion. Informal medical practitioners, including retired doctors, nurses, and medical students from refugee or diaspora communities, often provide services at reduced costs while maintaining cultural sensitivity and language compatibility. Often, these practitioners operate without official recognition, creating legal vulnerabilities while providing some essential services to excluded populations. Their work demonstrates how professional skills from homeland contexts can be adapted to serve refugee community needs, but also shows that qualifications are often not recognized, creating further vulnerabilities. Religious and ethnic networks also provide crucial healthcare support, with mosques, churches, and community organizations establishing informal medical assistance programs frequently staffed by refugee supporters in Malaysian society or by sympathetic expatriates with medical knowledge. For example, the Alliance of Chin Refugees (ACR), a major Chin refugee community coalition, had a medical clinic attached to its offices for a number of years, staffed by an expatriate Australian nurse, who had heard about refugees while living in Malaysia. Her husband had been posted to Kuala Lumpur, and she had expertise and time to contribute, and after meeting some Chin refugees helped set up the clinic. In the Klang Valley, Rohingya communities often receive mobile clinics staffed by medical and nursing students from local medical colleges. These impromptu visits help alleviate immediate need and offer basic check-ups, but cannot provide critical care. The Buddhist Tzu Chi organization from Taiwan operates one of the few clinics in Kuala Lumpur that offer general and dental care to refugees. Many of these initiatives operate through personal relationships between refugees and sympathetic Malaysian healthcare workers who provide pro bono services or facilitate access to reduced-cost treatment. The effectiveness of these networks depends on maintaining discretion while building trust across ethnic and religious boundaries.

Healthcare-seeking journeys themselves become part of a broader geography of exclusion and adaptation that shapes refugee life in the city. Accessing even informal medical care requires careful navigation through urban spaces where refugees must constantly negotiate their visibility. Thus, navigating urban space in Kuala Lumpur requires refugees to develop strategies for moving through a city designed to exclude their presence while facilitating their economic exploitation. These spatial strategies reveal both the constraints imposed by legal precarity and the creative ways refugees negotiate urban territory to maintain livelihoods, relationships, and community connections. Refugee mobility patterns in Kuala Lumpur reflect a complex calculus that balances economic necessity with arrest risk, creating distinctive geographies of movement that differ markedly from those of citizens. Many refugees concentrate their activities within specific neighborhoods where their presence is tolerated or normalized, while avoiding areas with heavy police presence or middle-class Malaysian residents who might report them to authorities. This spatial segregation creates informal refugee enclaves within the broader urban landscape.

Refugee mobility, meanwhile, follows careful temporal patterns, with early morning and late evening travel offering safer passage when the police presence is diminished. Transportation poverty compounds these constraints as refugees cannot afford private vehicles, and public transport stations become enforcement targets. Police routinely patrol monorail, bus, and train stations, knowing undocumented migrants rely on these services. This forces refugees to walk long distances or use expensive alternatives, such as Grab and taxis, particularly for essential services like medical appointments or UNHCR visits. Employment geography intensifies these challenges, as reaching construction sites, factories, and domestic work in affluent neighborhoods requires traveling significant distances while maintaining low visibility. This dispersion of work opportunities across Kuala Lumpur's periphery means transport costs can consume wages while arrest risks shape their every journey, effectively limiting refugees to jobs within a shorter distance or forcing them to accept diminished earnings and higher risks.

MAKING A LIFE BY MAKING A LIVING: SOLIDARITY, SUPPORT, AND MUTUALITY

Economic survival for refugees in Kuala Lumpur requires the daily navigation of complex informal labor markets where exploitation and opportunity coexist within relationships of mutual dependence between refugee workers and Malaysian employers. Excluded from formal employment, refugees accept dangerous, poorly paid work that nonetheless provides essential labor for Malaysia's development. The construction industry has emerged as a primary employer of refugee men, offering relatively high wages for physically demanding work while requiring no documentation beyond basic identity verification. Many construction sites operate with minimal government oversight, creating spaces where refugee labor can remain invisible to immigration authorities while contributing to Malaysia's urban development. The industry's demand for temporary workers aligns with refugee legal uncertainty, though working conditions are often dangerous and exploitative (Muniandy 2021). How precarious this kind of work can be was brought home to me through a particularly egregious story of how workers are treated. In 2012 and 2015, I visited a Catholic-run convalescent home about an hour outside Kuala Lumpur. There, some nuns and Catholic lay people offer respite to sick people, end-of-life care, and attend to some community members with severe disabilities. A nurse at the convalescent home told me about a Chin refugee lying in a bed, staring at the ceiling while a fan moved stale warm air around the silent room. The man had been a construction worker in Kuala Lumpur until he fell from scaffolding at a substantial height. The fall nearly killed him. He survived the emergency treatment but remained in a coma, unable to move, with doctors uncertain whether he would ever wake again. His wife and three children were devastated. The hospital costs mounted rapidly, but the construction company denied that he had ever worked for them and refused any assistance. The refugee community and church stepped in to help, eventually moving him to the convalescent home. The family was registered with UNHCR, which helped coordinate initial church support but could offer little else. Then came what should have been a moment of hope and joy: the family was approved for resettlement to the United States. But with the father still comatose, he could not travel. The family faced an impossible choice: the mother and children could accept resettlement and leave him behind, alone in Malaysia, or they could all remain, forgoing their chance at resettlement while struggling without income or prospects. They chose to go. Now the man lies in that bed, thousands of kilometers from his family in America, thousands of kilometers from his homeland in Myanmar, alone in a strange country under a slowly turning fan. This story captures both the callousness with which migrant workers are treated, essentially as nothing more than disposable bodies whose injuries are disavowed, and the cruel arithmetic forced upon refugees, where even opportunities for a new life in safety can require unbearable sacrifice.

Refugees cannot escape these realities, though, because they must earn their own money to survive. To do so, street vending and small-scale commerce offer refugees opportunities to develop independent economic activities while serving consumer needs within and outside refugee communities. Food stalls, phone card sales, remittance services, and small retail operations enable some refugees to utilize their homeland business experience while building customer relationships within urban neighborhoods. However, these activities require careful negotiation with local authorities and established vendors who may view refugees as unwelcome competition. The restaurant industry provides another major employment sector, particularly for refugees with culinary skills from their home countries. Many of the famous restaurant strips (especially those with Chinese restaurants) in Kuala Lumpur's tourist center and surrounding suburbs actually have refugee cooks and waiters. I interviewed a number of waiters and cooks in Jalan Alor, in the heart of the golden triangle, the busiest evening food street in Kuala Lumpur. They worked the usual long hours, but because they were given a place to stay above the restaurant, its central location meant they were well placed to take advantage of refugee community services and medical services of the nearby Tzu Chi clinic. Nonetheless, they also described the setup as predatory—their earnings were immediately docked to pay for the very expensive, very basic accommodations (owned by the restaurateur), meaning they actually earned very little in the end. In nearby Pudu, an old Chinese neighborhood, many Chinese restaurants and food courts also employ mostly Chin and Zomi refugees, who likewise live in the shop lots above the restaurants and old printing shops. Here, refugees feel relatively safe, having established themselves as a strong community that can wear their traditional dress to church on Sundays and carry their children in colorful cloth slings on their backs without harassment. But this is the exception.

How refugees get treated at their workplaces largely depends on the supervisors, owners, or bosses who are in charge. For example, one Rohingya refugee described how religious discrimination can intersect with economic vulnerability in the workplace:

> I say, "Boss, give me five times to pray." He say, "Cannot. I can only give you Friday prayer." So I think I cannot work, even my family in trouble now....

> There is no halal item. So I need to cook myself, I eat myself. Because at that time, I have nothing. I was documentless.... "Bodoh orang [stupid person]. Gila orang [crazy person]. Why you came here? Go now." (Rohingya interlocutor, fieldwork interview, November 23, 2016)

FIGURE 9 Daily life in Pudu, where many refugees live, work, and shop

Manufacturing employment, particularly in textile and electronics assembly, offers regular wages and structured working conditions, though often with minimal worker protections and below-market compensation. These jobs require refugees to present some documentation and maintain low profiles within factory environments where Malaysian workers may view them as threatening job security. Some refugees develop valuable technical skills that increase their employment options, though legal restrictions usually prevent career advancement.

The development of refugee-to-refugee economic networks creates alternative labor markets that operate independently of Malaysian oversight while serving community needs. Refugees with specific skills often provide services to other refugees, either in kinship-mediated markets or ethnically bounded groups. More often than not, traditional objects are produced for a touristic or expatriate market, as this allows small-scale producers to achieve the best prices. Several weaving collectives, sewing enterprises, and not-for-profit small-scale producers of food and knick-knacks will sell their wares at international school fetes, UNHCR-organized events, or other markets aimed at expatriates. These small-scale economies enable skill utilization (especially traditional ones, such as weaving and clothing) and income generation while also building community cohesion. Remittance labor is a category of refugee work in which individuals primarily focus on earning money to send to family members remaining in home countries or refugee camps. These workers often accept extremely low wages and poor working conditions in order to maximize remittance amounts, creating vulnerabilities that employers may exploit while generating crucial income for extended family networks.

Another major issue for refugees is finding suitable and affordable accommodation. Access to housing, especially in a city like Kuala Lumpur, requires complex negotiations of the conditional hospitality that characterizes refugee relationships with Malaysian society, where accommodation is available but contingent upon maintaining invisibility, accepting exploitation, and navigating landlord discretion. The concentration of refugees in specific urban neighborhoods reflects both economic necessity and the tolerance of particular Malaysian communities for refugee presence. Areas such as Selayang, Cheras, and parts of Kuala Lumpur's older residential districts have become informal refugee housing markets where landlords knowingly rent to undocumented populations while charging premium rates for often substandard accommodation.

Landlord attitudes toward refugee tenants vary considerably, ranging from exploitative profiteering to genuine humanitarian concern, with most relationships falling somewhere between these extremes. Some landlords view refugees as reliable tenants who pay rent promptly and cause minimal problems, while others see them as vulnerable populations from whom extra profits can be extracted through security deposits, utility surcharges, or threats of reporting to authorities. The development of refugee housing networks often operates through ethnic and religious connections, with established residents helping newcomers locate accommodation while vouching for their reliability to suspicious landlords. These networks create clusters of refugees from particular regions or ethnic groups within specific buildings or neighborhoods, enabling mutual support while potentially increasing visibility to enforcement authorities. Shared accommodation proves essential for most refugees, who cannot afford individual rental properties and require community support for daily survival. Multiple families often share a single apartment, with sleeping areas allocated according to shift work schedules and family size. These arrangements require careful negotiation of privacy, cleanliness, and resource sharing while managing the social tensions that arise from overcrowding and economic stress. Usually, rooms are subdivided with wooden panels into areas with just enough space for sleeping mats for family members, while basic cooking facilities and bathrooms are shared.

FIGURE 10 Home-based tailoring work is a common income-generating activity for refugee women

The entrepreneurial adaptation to housing constraints is embodied in Komar Jahan's remarkable transformation from tenant to landlord (based on fieldwork interviews conducted in November 2015). When we met her, Komar was 50 years old, had been in Malaysia for 26 years, and had navigated the complexities of the housing market to create her own subletting enterprise while maintaining her primary income as a roadside betel nut seller near Selayang Market. Komar Jahan's housing journey began when she arrived in Malaysia in 1989, fleeing Burma after the 1988 demonstrations and escaping an unhappy marriage. "I will come to Malaysia, I will enjoy my life here, I will do whatever I want to do," she declared to her disapproving parents, embodying an independence that would characterize her entire Malaysian experience. After working in restaurants for years, she established her betel nut business, learning the craft from her first husband, who owned a large shop in Rangoon. This shift to self-employment provided the foundation for her later housing entrepreneurship.

For the past four years, she rented an entire floor of a five-story shophouse in Selayang for RM 1,000 per month, subletting six rooms to other Rohingya refugees. She charges RM 180 per person or RM 250 per couple, generating income at full occupancy that exceeds her costs, though utilities add approximately RM 400 per month. Her current tenants include two single men who have lived there since she first rented the property, a single mother with five children, and, intermittently, two teenage girls whose mother moved to Ampang but who prefer the freedom of Selayang. "They are like my children," Komar Jahan explained, noting how the girls provide company for her own 18-year-old daughter.

Her preference for controlling the entire floor rather than renting individual rooms reflects her strategic thinking: "I prefer to rent the whole level and find tenants because if I am the lease-holder, it is more comfortable, I can choose the people who live there. If I rent just a room from a landlord, I will have to follow someone else's rules." This arrangement provides both economic benefit and social control, enabling her to create a household environment aligned with her values while generating income.

The precariousness underlying her seeming success becomes apparent in her confrontation with the Myanmar Muslim landlord, who, in turn, rents from a Chinese property owner. When she first took the lease, the house was filthy and unwanted, renting for just RM 800. After she cleaned and improved it, the landlord raised the rent to RM 950, then RM 1,000. As she continued making repairs and improvements, he attempted to reclaim the property in its entirety. To fight the eviction, Komar Jahan consulted a "powerful man" who controls that area of Selayang, who then informed the landlord that any attempt to reclaim the property would have to go through him. She boldly told the landlord he could have the property back when she left for resettlement to the United States (in her imagined future). "I think he is now afraid of me," she said with evident satisfaction.

FIGURE 11 Light well in an apartment building housing multiple refugee families

Yet this entrepreneurial success coexists with profound vulnerability. During a police raid, officers cut through her security door when she did not open it quickly enough, leaving it unable to lock. She has fallen from buildings twice, injuring herself in the process. Once, fleeing from immigration officers, she fell and was left with chronic injuries that make sitting uncomfortable and walking painful. She works relentlessly, returning home at 1 or 2 a.m. from her betel nut stall, waking at 5 a.m. for morning prayers, then undertaking household chores. "I have no time to think, no time to sit," she explained, laughing. "I am always rushing between chores and work."

The emotional toll of family separation adds another layer of precarity. Her eldest daughter was resettled to the United States in January 2015, leaving her youngest daughter bereft. During our interview, Komar Jahan suddenly began crying: "My youngest daughter is often alone at home. My eldest daughter has been resettled to the U.S., and the younger daughter often cries because she misses her." Her three sons from her first marriage live in Malaysia but maintain little contact with her. "My sons in Malaysia are married and do not take care of me; I cannot depend on them for anything, and I feel that they do not think of me," she said with resignation.

Komar Jahan's subletting operation thus exemplifies the complex reality of refugee housing entrepreneurship. She has transformed precarity into enterprise, converting knowledge of the housing market and accumulated social capital into economic opportunity. Yet this success remains contingent upon her continued physical capacity to work multiple jobs, her strategic deployment of powerful intermediaries, and the absence of police action that might dismantle her carefully constructed domestic economy.

Such subletting arrangements enable some refugees to access housing through intermediary tenants who hold formal lease agreements with property owners. These arrangements often involve Malaysian citizens or documented migrants who rent properties and then subdivide them for refugee occupation, creating layers of rental relationships that provide plausible deniability for property owners while generating profit for intermediaries. The quality of refugee housing varies dramatically based on economic capacity and landlord attitudes, ranging from decent apartments rented at market rates to severely overcrowded rooms lacking basic amenities. Many refugee families live in spaces without adequate ventilation, sanitation, or privacy, accepting these conditions because alternatives remain unavailable or unaffordable. Security deposits and advance rent payments create additional barriers for refugees seeking housing, as landlords often demand multiple months' payment upfront to compensate for the perceived risks of renting to undocumented tenants. These requirements force refugees to accumulate substantial savings before moving, limiting housing mobility while creating opportunities for exploitation.

One Rohingya refugee described the vulnerability to sudden eviction without dignity:

> One black man, Indian maybe. The woman is Malay, the manager; the black Indian roughly said, "You need to get out now." I could not say anything. I say something, they become more cruel. So, I am afraid.... They did not give us any dignity, right? They said, "Get out now. The house has been sold.'" (fieldwork interview, December 2, 2016)

Neighborhood integration varies considerably depending on local Malaysian attitudes toward refugee presence, with some communities developing cooperative relationships while others remain suspicious or hostile. Successful integration often depends on refugees maintaining low profiles while contributing positively to local commerce and social life. Children playing with Malaysian neighbors, families shopping at local markets, and refugees participating in community religious activities can foster acceptance, but this is not a given. The development of informal housing assistance networks within refugee communities demonstrates remarkable mutual aid and resource sharing. Families facing eviction may receive temporary accommodation from community members. These networks, therefore, can create safety nets that can substitute for formal social services.

The refugee-to-refugee assistance networks that provide this safety net often operate through spontaneous acts of recognition and compassion rather than formal organizational structures. Komar Jahan's support of Aminah, a young Rohingya mother, exemplifies how these informal solidarities function in practice. Their relationship began one night approximately seven months before our interview, when Komar Jahan saw Aminah arrive in Selayang with four children and nowhere to stay. Aminah had just been released from a trafficking camp in Thailand, separated from her husband, and knew no one in the area. These camps had become horrifyingly common along the Thai-Malaysian border. In May 2015, the discovery of mass graves at Wang Kelian on the Thai-Malaysian border exposed the brutal reality of human trafficking networks that had operated with impunity for years. Malaysian authorities exhumed 139 bodies from shallow graves in jungle trafficking camps where rape, torture, and murder were systematically employed against Rohingya refugees (Menon 2015). These camps functioned as extortion centers where refugees who had fled Myanmar, believing they were paying for safe passage to Malaysia, were instead imprisoned in bamboo cages and held for ransom. Those unable to pay faced starvation, beatings, and death. The trafficking networks operated with the tacit approval of authorities on both sides of the border. The Wang Kelian graves revealed not just individual tragedies but the structural violence of a system where desperate refugees fleeing genocide in Myanmar became commodities in a brutal economy of exploitation, their bodies discarded in unmarked graves when their value as sources of ransom was exhausted. Aminah had survived such a camp, but her husband remained missing, his fate unknown.

"I felt a lot of pity for the children because they were in very poor health," Komar Jahan explained. Her son suggested they offer Aminah a room, and Komar Jahan agreed despite her own financial constraints. The assistance she provides extends beyond accommodation. She shares food when she can, though she makes no promises about daily provisions. She also took Aminah to a clinic for a pregnancy test after noticing signs. Aminah had become pregnant while in the trafficking camp with her husband. These camps are notorious for the rape and torture of Rohingya, who are often held captive until family and friends can pay the ransom. Aminah's children, especially an eight-year-old daughter and six-year-old son, contribute what they can by collecting bottles and cans near Komar Jahan's betel nut stall, earning two or three *ringgit* that help buy necessities. Sometimes locals give the children small amounts of money when they see them playing nearby. This small income supplements whatever assistance Komar Jahan can provide and whatever money Aminah's mother in Myanmar can occasionally send by selling land.

This relationship exposes important dimensions of refugee mutual aid networks. First, the support crosses village lines, as Aminah later clarified that she and Komar Jahan are not from the same village in Myanmar, contrary to my initial assumptions. Their connection was forged entirely through the chance encounter in Selayang, demonstrating that refugee solidarity can transcend pre-existing ties. Second, the assistance operates without formal expectations of reciprocity. Komar Jahan provides housing to Aminah, knowing she may never be repaid, and Aminah contributes labor whenever possible without an explicit agreement. Third, the support remains fundamentally precarious. Komar Jahan's own economic situation is unstable, as evidenced by her concern about rent when tenants leave. Her ability to continue supporting Aminah depends entirely on her continued employment and housing security.

For Aminah, this informal support means survival. She cannot access the UNHCR because she lacks documentation. In fact, they turned her away when she tried to visit their office, as at the time all refugees from Myanmar required a pre-arranged appointment to see the UNHCR. In addition, she has no social network in Malaysia beyond Komar Jahan. Aminah remains without her husband, not even knowing whether he is still alive; she also reminisced about her reliance on him for her social life and network. Aminah explained, "[In Myanmar,] I largely stayed at home and did not know many people.... I was very reliant on my husband." Her former domestic isolation has translated into profound vulnerability in Malaysia, where navigating urban space, finding employment, and accessing services all require networks and knowledge she lacks. Thus, Komar's support also has profound emotional dimensions, which prove equally significant. When Aminah's children ask for better food, such as fish, curry, or other things they see other people eating, she cannot provide it, and this inability causes her profound sadness. Komar Jahan's willingness to share what she has, even when it is very little, provides not just material assistance but recognition and dignity. The informal kinship ties they have created, with teenage girls from other tenants playing with Aminah's children and Komar Jahan taking on a maternal role, partially substitute for the family networks that typically provide such support.

This relationship between Komar Jahan and Aminah illustrates the essential function of informal refugee support networks. Such networks enable survival for the most vulnerable refugees, who fall through the cracks of formal assistance systems or who cannot access them due to documentation issues. Yet they also redistribute precarity rather than eliminating it, transferring risk and responsibility from formal institutions to refugees who themselves live in constant insecurity. This creation of largely invisible support networks represents perhaps the most remarkable aspect of refugee urban survival, demonstrating how displaced populations can and do develop systems of mutual aid, resource sharing, and collective protection that often prove more responsive and effective than formal humanitarian assistance. These networks operate through multiple channels (ethnic, religious, geographic), creating overlapping webs of support that provide resilience against the various crises that characterize refugee life.

Childcare networks, as evidenced in Komar's relationship to Aminah's children, for example, enable refugee parents to secure and maintain employment while ensuring children receive supervision and even informal education during working hours. Extended family members, community elders, and trusted neighbors often provide childcare services without formal payment, creating reciprocal care systems that support family economic survival while building intergenerational community connections (Lamb and Hoffstaedter 2020). In addition, cultural preservation networks maintain homeland traditions, languages, and practices through community celebrations, religious observances, and cultural education programs (see chapter 7). These activities provide psychological support and identity maintenance while creating opportunities for intergenerational knowledge transfer.

Religious spaces can be particularly important sites of refugee place-making as outlined in previous chapters, where community members gather for worship, cultural celebration, and mutual support. This is particularly true for churches in Malaysia's Myanmar Christian communities, as congregations are usually from cohesive linguistic and ethnic groups. Muslim refugees tend to attend neighborhood mosques and must learn Malay to understand sermons; while some mosques with high refugee congregations may develop special programs and services that address community needs, most do not.

FIGURE 12 Fellowship service at a church supporting a Chin refugee community in Kuala Lumpur

So, while there are severe constraints, refugees in Kuala Lumpur do create meaningful urban lives that transcend mere survival. The growth of communities through marriage and having children represents perhaps the most profound act of hope, despite their uncertain legal status. As one Malaysian-born Rohingya refugee expressed: "I feel it is my home … because I was born here." Another long-term resident captured the complexity of belonging without acceptance: "We feel that we've been here for long. Maybe it's here? Don't know. But if we're given a chance, we would like to live here because we've been here since small. But if we don't get accepted, what choice do we have?"

The networks refugees create, from Komar Jahan's subletting arrangements to informal education systems, demonstrate remarkable resilience and innovation in addressing their community needs. These networks often prove more responsive than formal services, revealing both the lack of state or civil society services and the potential of community-based mutual aid. Through religious gatherings, cultural celebrations, and commercial enterprises, refugees transform anonymous urban spaces into sites of belonging, asserting claims to urban territory while building bridges with Malaysian communities.

The dialectics of visibility and invisibility that characterize refugee experience manifest the topolganger logic described above: refugees must be visible enough to access work and services while sufficiently invisible to maintain the unseeing that allows them to exist in spaces the state claims to control. This process of unseeing and invisibility demands constant vigilance; this permanent hypervigilance exacts high psychological costs for refugees.

The topolganger logic that structures daily life in Kuala Lumpur creates a peculiar form of belonging in which refugees are simultaneously present and absent, visible and invisible, integrated and excluded. They participate fully in urban economic life while being systematically denied urban political life. This spatial arrangement serves multiple interests: employers gain cheap labor, landlords collect premium rents, the state maintains plausible deniability about refugee presence, and refugees themselves carve out spaces of relative safety through strategic invisibility. Yet this arrangement remains fundamentally unstable, vulnerable to breaches stemming from enforcement crackdowns, policy changes, public health crises, or simply the accumulated visibility that comes from refugees building lives, raising children, and claiming space over time.

Ultimately, being a refugee in Malaysia means living a contradiction: meaningful participation in city life occurs alongside systematic exclusion through a lack of legal recognition. Through their place-making practices, economic contributions, and community networks, refugees demonstrate that urban belonging transcends formal citizenship or legal rights to be there. Their achievements deserve recognition not as exceptional stories of resilience but as evidence that even within hostile environments, displaced populations create systems of support, meaning, and hope that often work better than official structures designed to exclude them. The question, therefore, is not whether refugees belong in the city; through their labor, their communities, and their children born here, they have already claimed Kuala Lumpur as their home. The real question is when Malaysian society will recognize what already exists. The next chapter delves deeper into a small but hopeful example of a lived alternative reality in which refugees are integrated into a small rural Malaysian community and feel accepted and sufficiently safe to go about their daily lives.

CHAPTER 6

Farming for a New Life

City and Rural Refugee Place-making in Peninsular Malaysia

On a hot and sultry afternoon, we are in the Malaysian jungle, not far from a refugee-run farm, making our way through the thicket. My gumboots are soaked with mud and muddy water as I scale another ridge, trying to keep up with Simon. Simon is hunting. He has set out traps for wild boar, and he is hopeful of catching this tasty prize once more—he has had some recent success and shared the wild boar meat with his wife and several other refugees from Myanmar living nearby. We come upon a clearing and a track that Simon has fashioned to guide the boar toward his trap. "Stop." Simon's hand grabs me from behind, just inches from the trap I had not seen—the trap is empty. No boar today. The trap is made of a cut-down tree, spring-loaded and tied to a noose on the ground, basic and ingenious. On our way back, we check another trap and hear some murmurs from the jungle. I stay back, armed with a stick. Simon wields a machete. Then laughter rings out, then concern, then shrieks. I turn the corner and see a clearing with a trap set out and a monkey sitting on the forest floor, shrieking in pain. The snare has caught the monkey's leg, and it looks infected. Simon tries to calm the monkey so he can free him, but the monkey fights back. Simon fashions a noose with some rope and ties it to a stick to detain the monkey so we can free its leg from the trap. The leg is injured, and we take the monkey back to the farmhouse, where Simon builds a makeshift cage for it and tends to the wound. The monkey quickly catches the attention of Simon's neighbors, and more than one person approaches him to buy it (to eat). Simon brushes them off, opting to keep the monkey and nurse him back to health so that he might become a hunting aide, especially to help cut coconuts from coconut palms.

FIGURE 13 Monkey caught in Simon's trap

BATU ARANG: BUILDING AN ALTER-COMMUNITY

In one day, following Simon around the farm and bush, multiple levels of place-making, dwelling, and belonging became apparent in a country that neither legally nor politically offers refugees any recognition, that in fact hounds and detains them whenever possible. This chapter builds on the theoretical framework of place-making under polycrisis conditions and describes how some refugees in Malaysia have found ways to escape the cycle of a life lived merely in legal limbo. I conducted several weeks of fieldwork research with refugees living on farms near Kuala Lumpur, where they have established a different way of life. Many refugees can make lives for themselves beyond mere survival; some even manage to flourish and make Malaysia their home, and while they continue to be denied the opportunity to live in an organic community of their own making, some are able to find and carve out spaces to engage in alter-politics (Hage 2015). For a number of years, the UNHCR maintained a Special Protection Fund that, between 2010 and 2012, awarded grants of RM 12,000 (USD 3,000) each to some refugee community groups in Malaysia to invest in livelihood measures. Through this measure, they supported three farming endeavors run by three different ethnically based refugee community organizations, including Karen, Rakhine, and Chin. Some of these farms started out elsewhere but, over time, migrated to Batu Arang, where, with the help of the local Catholic Church, farmland could be more easily rented. Now all three are situated within walking distance of each other on the outskirts of Batu Arang.

FIGURE 14 Refugee farm in Batu Arang, northwest of Kuala Lumpur

The fieldsite of Batu Arang, around 50 km northwest of Kuala Lumpur, is home to many smallholdings and some organic and permaculture farms. Some are run by city types seeking a tree change or progressive lifestyle, while others are run by an array of individuals trying to make a living off the land. Batu Arang is also of broader historical importance in Malaysia. In the early part of the twentieth century, the town was a coal mining area that delivered vital fuel for energy production and to the Malayan railway system, which linked the British colonies of Singapore and Penang and delivered tin and rubber to the coast. The collieries themselves were huge, leaving behind hollowed-out hillsides and open pits to this day:

> The vast domain of Malayan Collieries at Batu Arang in Selangor was a state within the state. Here the management saw its elaborate controls over a 6,000-strong workforce as modern and enlightened. But it was also a place where workers' indebtedness under the contract system was most severe. (Bayly and Harper 2005, 42)

On several occasions, predominantly Chinese workers went on strike, demanding better conditions, most notably in 1936, 1937, and 1947. In 1937, a brief soviet government was established, and workers were able to pressure the government with strikes that also affected Malaya's main power supply. The large-scale protests that shook the Malay Peninsula at this time tore through plantations, rubber estates, and mines until "the Batu Arang Soviet was crushed ruthlessly by 250 police and 200 Malay troops. They shot one worker and injured four more. Lacking citizenship, hundreds were banished to China" (Bayly and Harper 2005, 42). The soviet had lasted only seven days.

Not much is left of Batu Arang's revolutionary past, although some locals still remember, in largely nostalgic terms, the coal-mining days and the wealth they created. There may also be a latent memory of resistance to the state and being outside the Malaysian state, if only for a short period of time, and this openness to the other may retain a powerful capacity to make room for others today. The Catholic Church is a major landowner in Batu Arang, dating back to early missionary work in the area. They maintain several HIV/AIDS shelters, convalescent homes, and vocational training centers in the area. The local parish is also supportive of refugee concerns, sometimes arranging funerals, which is especially difficult for undocumented people in Malaysia. The town applied to the Selangor state government for heritage town status, receiving it in 2011; it has since revived tourism in the area through its heritage trail, which traces its coal-mining history. Since the demise of coal operations, the last industrial remnant is an ordnance factory on the outskirts of town, but the population is now largely an older demographic that appreciates the rich history, runs small farms, and enjoys retirement.

One particular local, Alex, had previously worked with the Catholic Church and was now running his own shelter. He supported the local refugee farms by signing the lease for the Karen farm and helping Simon with his attempts at organic farming; Alex hoped the "organic" distinction would make the crops more marketable, especially in selling them to parishioners after church services in Kuala Lumpur, which Alex also helped with. He was a member of a minority ethnic group in Malaysia and thus himself somewhat marginalized vis-à-vis the Malaysian state. This, coupled with a radical Catholic religiosity that was informed by liberation theology and its commitment to praxis and actively helping the poor, may go some way to explain his actions, but it must be noted that this form of refugee advocate in Malaysia remains the exception—a shared marginality does not necessarily compel people to transversal solidarity and action. Nonetheless, the church infrastructure and faith play an enormous role in the placement and sustainability of the farms. Alex is a savvy guide who helps steer refugees in their local endeavors; such guides are crucial to successfully navigating new worlds and the relationships they form there. The impact can be immediate: for example, when Simon needed some form of mulch to cover his budding plants on the farm, Alex put him in touch with a local contractor mowing the roadsides in Batu Arang. We spent the next day collecting and ferrying back bales of cut grass for Simon to use. This kind of community support helps the farms and allows refugee farmers to live within the community as active members, rather than as pariahs, as they do in the city. This visibility and active engagement with locals can also, to some degree, protect them from the authorities, as it shows them as active and productive members of the community.

Simon and Mary lived and worked on the Chin farm. He is an ethnic Chin from Hakha Township in Chin State, in northwestern Myanmar, who fled in 2007 during the increasing army atrocities there. His family was a farming family and had a plot of land in their village, where they largely grew rice. Simon helped farm the family plot and took on work for neighbors in their permanent gardens. He was intimately connected to the land his family and ancestors had worked, mostly for swidden agriculture. The Chin Hills were and are contested territory, and his family was often caught in the crossfire between the Chin National Front (CNF) and the Myanmar army, as the CNF had a base nearby. "In our village, rebels ask for money as does the Myanmar military, as well as portering work and other forced labor, so I left," Simon told me. Many Chin have been subject to forced labor and conscription into portering duties for the Myanmar military over the years of conflict in Chin State. Portering entails carrying large 25 kg bags of rice through mountainous terrain to supply army units, while porters were often beaten and inadequately fed.

In 2007, Simon reached Mae Sai, Thailand, in the Golden Triangle, and stayed in Bangkok for two years. There he met Mary, who is from Shan State and had fled Myanmar in 2008. Her village in Shan State had experienced similar land grabs and dispossessions as Simon's, and she recounted how her family's big gardens close to town were taken over by the military;

her family was ordered to work on their own land for their new masters or face exorbitant fines. In these circumstances, local vegetables and staples are often replaced by cash crops such as jatropha, which the army can sell for foreign currency. "We were forced to destroy all our crops and work on our own land [by the army]." Having to work on land that used to be your own leaves little time to find food to survive, and in 2008, she fled to Thailand, reaching Bangkok mid-year. Shortly after she met Simon, they got married in Bangkok. They were unaware of the UNHCR or the protection it can afford refugees in Thailand, believing community rumors that the UNHCR is only for Karen people. Thus, they moved on to Malaysia in the hope of better protection and a new life. They remained unregistered on the farm for several years, having missed a major UNHCR registration drive when they arrived in 2012.

Before arriving on the Chin farm, Mary and Simon both lived in Sungai Besi, an urban township of Kuala Lumpur, but struggled to find work. Mary worked as a dishwasher for a time, and Simon did odd jobs, but they could barely survive in the city due to relatively high rents and living costs. Working on the farm provided them with a regular income from the refugee community organization. The organization also provided Simon with seeds to plant, and after the harvest, he would give them the produce to sell in Kuala Lumpur. As they had just started the farm when I arrived, the gardens were still small and expanding, with young plants growing steadily along the plastic lines laid out for them. When I asked him what the main difference was between living in the city and the countryside, a smile flickered across his face. "In the city, life is hard every day. No job, no time, no life." On the farm, he could be with his wife all day and replicate a life long lost in Myanmar, but one they both seemed nostalgic about. The nostalgia was not about farming per se, but about the environment, a green outlook, wandering the bush, and a feeling of security in moving about the small town. Here on the farm, husband and wife tended to the garden together, setting and shoring up the rigging to secure the poles for the structures that would support a crop of beans. With the harvest three months away, the shoots were already creeping up the plastic strings to the top, although the seeds smuggled in from Myanmar seemed to be growing faster and lusher than the local seeds, according to Simon. He proudly remarked that the Myanmar seeds required very few nutrients and were much hardier than the local ones.

FIGURE 15 Bean cultivation on a refugee farm

What refugees working on the farm were doing was settling land in a country that does not otherwise afford them a place. This act of settlement is important as it signals a level of agency among refugees and an ability to circumvent the state, which sees this sort of place-making as an affront to the logic of the Malaysian nation and the place of the refugee within it. And yet these examples do not sufficiently speak of the complexity and multiplicity of the refugee lifeworld and their experiences, in part because it is, as one refugee farmer told me, "unspeakable hard" to live in a state of limbo, with many family responsibilities and no rights to anything. So unspeakable is the trauma many refugees carry with them that they do not speak of the hardship they encountered in their home countries when they fled in the first place, let alone the hardship they encounter in Malaysia. As one Chin refugee put it: "The situation here is unspeakable, but more so not heard." What sustains many refugees is hope; as one Karen woman remarked, "Hope is that we can be resettled and our children can be well educated, we can work there." This utopian dream of the "good life" in a safe third (resettlement) country sustains them in urban contexts where they remain contained and fearful (Kleist and Jansen 2016).

The power of dwelling in both Malaysia and Myanmar at the same time is always palpable in soccer matches between hometown teams among the Chin community, for example. The way ideas and affective attachments to home travel with refugees extends beyond a locality and into the family and extended kin groups. As such, these identifiers may be conceptualized as concentric circles of self, family, kin, and the wider refugee community to which every refugee belongs. Kinship itself is a powerful trope, and many stories told to me harked back to the family members left behind in Myanmar and projected to the (better) lives of those already resettled in the West. Kinship not only plays a role in replicating refugee community structures as explained above, but is also a potent metaphor for how people reconnect with others sharing a particular experience, in this case, the refugee experience in Malaysia. This can happen with actual kin relations, such as Simon and his wife Mary (with a baby on the way), or with imagined or fictive kin networks, such as were present on the Karen farm next door.

There, a range of people are given some respite from the precarity of being predominantly urban refugees. The Karen refugee organization employs a family consisting of a grandmother and her daughter to manage the farm. Karen refugees in need of respite, such as pregnant or post-delivery women, recovering drug addicts, long-term ill, mentally ill, and those with no job find a temporary home on this Karen farm. Many stay only a couple of days if they cannot deal with the isolation of Batu Arang, a three-hour bus ride from Kuala Lumpur with three changes. Others stay for weeks, months, or even years. While I was there, two young women had arrived. They had no job and had only just arrived in Malaysia, so the Karen refugee organization placed them on the farm for a while until they could find them jobs. There, they helped with household chores and preparing vegetables for sale, finding their places in the makeshift family at the farm. The imagined family structure and support network that came with it built resilience, coping mechanisms, and a sense of belonging to a revolving group of people who shared deep connections through language, ethnicity, and/or culture.

The quiet rhythms of farm life—foraging for mussels along flooded mine lakes, sharing meals across neighboring plots, sitting and chatting with friends over instant coffee as the day ends—offered something rarely available in the city: the simple, restorative act of being present without fear. On the farms in Batu Arang, refugees were, for a moment, just neighbors and friends, absorbed in the mundane and ordinary business of the day. The wider world and their precarious position in it, their legal limbo, the state surveillance, and the threat of arrest all receded from here.

Thus, the contrast between city life and farm life could not be starker. In the city, refugees have to be constantly attentive, scanning and aware of the state scanning for them (police, immigration officers, etc.). On the farm, they feel less exhausted from the constant fear of detection and anxiety about others. Here, they can relax to the extent possible, let their guard down, and regain some emotional capacity to be human beings engaged in life. There is a sense of motionless drifting or being marooned far from home(land) and far from the state's grasp of domination (Hobsbawm 1990; Price 1996). In the city, camouflage and concealment are the dominant modes of being—a rhizomatic form of being that maintains identity and otherness underground. On the farms, the rhizome is allowed to pierce society's surface and develop. Similarly, Richard Price uncovers the deep histories and engagements so-called maroons, or escaped slaves, have had and how they (re-) established communities "from scratch" (Price 1990, 1996) and

> today, when such peoples continue to be threatened by repressive national governments [...] they fight on, refusing to forget their collective past and insisting on their own right to define themselves and their world. (Price 2005, 65)

Simon and Mary find the farm work resonates with their former lives in Myanmar before the army confiscated their land, imbuing it with significance their urban survival work lacked. The farm allots them a life beyond survival and simultaneously allows them to envisage a new life. The monkey Simon caught earlier thus becomes an integral part of a new form of refugee place-making that includes remnants of the Malaysian wild bush and its untamed inhabitants (the monkey and the wild boar). The boar provides sustenance (survival) while the monkey represents possibilities beyond survival in the form of reciprocity (hoping the monkey will work with Simon to collect coconuts) or even mutuality (taking care of and tending to the monkey). The latter was exemplified by Simon sitting by the cage for hours and talking soothingly to the monkey, apologizing for its capture, applying cream to its wound, and feeding it fresh fruit. For Simon and Mary, the farm further provided a place outside the Malaysian state's purview and its attempts to capture those it deems illegal immigrants. Both noted how the village allowed them far more mobility, enabling regular weekend market visits and social calls to neighbors on adjacent plots, a mix of Myanmar guest workers and other refugees. Indeed, one concern often reported to me by urban refugees in Kuala Lumpur was that they were too scared to venture outside for fear of immigration or police officers. They complained, "We're not happy at all—as a human being we have to be free." On the farm, much more of this freedom to move without peril and fear was evident.

The working of the land, in the form of tilling with rudimentary tools and forming garden beds from bare soil, signaled a transformative power. One day, we were digging grooves to irrigate the seedlings, and over the course of a couple of days, we completely transformed a flat brown field into a series of orderly rows, ready for the bean seedlings. Further, at the back of the property, Simon extended a bed for betel leaves to be grown and supplied to the city. Betel leaves are important to many people from Myanmar, as they chew betel nut, which can be purchased from roadside vendors in suburbs with high numbers of refugee and migrant residents. Some of the ingredients are grown on these farms and provide a good cash crop (entirely outside the state economy), sold to consumers through a refugee-led and -owned supply chain. Such farm work enables refugees to forge direct connections with the land, an engagement typically forbidden to non-citizens in Malaysia.

This form of place-making fundamentally challenges national logics that position refugees as perpetually outside permitted forms of national belonging. The farms create dual resonances: connecting refugees to Malaysian soil while simultaneously evoking their former agricultural lives in Myanmar. These spaces thus open multiple possibilities for dwelling and establishing what might be called, following Heidegger's formulation, a *domus*, or a home grounded in the relationship between person, structure, and land itself (Heidegger 1971). However provisional or imagined, this domus offers refugees a space of safety and rootedness, i.e., a connection to the mythical *Heimat* that resonates particularly for those with peasant backgrounds.

FIGURE 16 Betel leaf cultivation on the Chin refugee farm near Batu Arang

Working on and with the land was qualitatively different from wage labor in the city for farmers like Simon. There, work was performed primarily to earn money and engage in the capitalist economy to ensure survival for oneself and one's family. Working on the land offered different opportunities to engage with people and the sociality of rural economies, where labor, goods, and services are exchanged, binding people together through the gift economy (Mauss [1954] 2002). This was exemplified by several encounters I witnessed between the refugee farmers and locals. On one occasion, I had just returned from the jungle, checking the wild boar traps with Simon, when a local Indian man approached on a motorbike. Draped across him and the bike was a massive python. He gestured for Simon to inspect the snake and said in English, "You eat?" Simon was unsure what was being offered and why, but it soon transpired that the man believed people from Myanmar ate snakes, and he wanted to trade the snake for some boar meat or other produce from Simon's farm. On this occasion, no deal was made as Simon declined the offer, but he had an ongoing exchange with the local milk supplier, who dropped off some milk every morning on his motorbike in exchange for eggs and other fresh produce. Therefore, the land provided a very material way of making home and place for them through their dwelling on and working of the land and using its produce to connect them to the people around them.

This is not to suggest that home can only be articulated in this way; indeed, it may be Eurocentric to equate the need for permanent dwellings with a sense of being at home in the world. Furthermore, Heidegger's later works themselves engage the poetry of Hölderlin, in which journeying and homecoming in the sense of a "return to the nearness of being" take center stage: "We dwell, and yet we do not dwell" (Malpas 2006, 309). Farms, I argue here, offer a place for refugees to engage in this sort of journeying to themselves; a place to make identity and themselves. Yet this connection between land and rootedness sits uneasily with historical realities in both highland Myanmar and the Malay world, where mobile populations and transportable dwellings were traditional patterns (Kahn 2006; Lehman 1963). Western colonialism and subsequent transformations in land tenure arrangements largely obliterated this heritage of movement. Still, territorialized notions of belonging continue to wield enormous symbolic and political force over Malaysia's national imagination and governance (Cheah Boon Kheng 2002). The *bumiputera* classification encompasses most Malaysians, including the dominant Malay population along with several East Malaysian Indigenous ethnic groups, all receiving affirmative action benefits. Malays particularly enjoy preferential property pricing and privileged access to designated Malay reserve lands in Peninsular Malaysia. Through these mechanisms, state policy inscribes an essentialized connection between Malay collective identity and territorial occupation, operating under explicitly nativist premises. Since before Malaysian independence in 1957, Malays have pursued a sense of ownership of the body politic, as the economy was seen as a largely Chinese domain. Both Chinese and Indian minorities have been relegated, at times, to *pendatang* (newcomer) or sojourners, which directly speaks to the imagined Malay position as the landowners and the heightened politics around land and indigeneity in Malaysia.

One place urban refugees rarely engage with, or even see, is the wild jungle that is rapidly vanishing in Malaysia, replaced by palm oil plantations and urban sprawl. Refugees from Myanmar used to squat in plantations and at the edges of the city in jungle camps until the mid-2000s, when the police were called in to clear the illegal squatters from government and corporately owned land (Nah 2010). The subsequent mass move into urban anonymity was accompanied by mass raids, detention of thousands of refugees, and renewed displacement. Nowadays, only a few refugees remain on far-flung plantations, laboring for a meager income and living in jungle camps. In the jungle, many refugees survived by hunting, gathering, and with the help of local NGOs and church groups that became aware of their plight. Once they had settled in the city, open spaces and hunting became things some urban refugees spoke about nostalgically. On the farms, there were opportunities to hone acquired skills, such as hunting, and Simon was fast becoming known for his talents in the neighborhood. He had already caught three wild boars in the three months he had been on the farm. Behind the Rakhine farm, jungle forest stretched out with ample gullies and freshwater sources. Here, wild boar run free, and Simon had built large traps for them. The last time his trap had successfully sprang into action was when he was about to go to the market to buy meat, as they had run out. He went to check the traps one last time and, he said, "Thanks to God's grace, there was a big boar." According to Simon, God had intervened and provided them with meat. The meat—boar is considered a delicacy in Chin State—was shared among the refugee community in Batu Arang. Often, other refugees commented on Simon's prowess as a hunter, noting that he had provided them with wild boar meat. The exchange economy and the ability to provide for oneself and others were other aspects that many refugees saw as distinguishing features of their life on the farms.

One refugee farmer told me, "I want to use my brain for myself here. If I go to work elsewhere, the boss is in charge. They come to my brain, and my body is like a machine. Do this! Do that!" He had worked on commercial farms before and in a factory and did not like the treatment he received, i.e., being bossed around. In that environment, he always felt "very pressured." He went on to explain that

> before I [was] a refugee, I can do what the boss tells me, because I am just looking for money. Now I am a refugee, I am conflicted. I have two feelings: pressure from the boss and pressure from being a refugee.

He contrasted this to being a migrant, who only feels pressure from their boss. As migrant laborers, they would have their passports and would be free to move. As refugees, they have no permit, no authority, and no legality, which all restrict them and put additional pressure on their lives. He tried to tell this to his former boss because he wanted him to understand what it is like to live as a working refugee; sadly, his former boss "did not understand" him. Refugees in Malaysia continue to be marginalized from society, which puts them in a much more precarious position outside the law. In the example above, a refugee was trying to get his employer to understand this difference, and the ensuing miscomprehension is, foremost, a commentary on the way most Malaysian employers perceive their undocumented workers: as only (cheap) labor, or what Muniandy (2021) has called "ghost labor." This is especially prevalent at the lower end of the skill base in Malaysia, where refugee workers often cannot communicate properly with their employers due to language barriers. It is also a commentary on the incommensurability of the world refugees inhabit with that of their employers.

Away from at least one of these pressures, Simon and several other refugee farmers regularly meet on Sunday, their day of rest, to read from the Bible, discuss Christianity, and their lives in Malaysia, as well as go to the market to get provisions they do not (yet) grow on the farm. These days are spent chatting, playing with the dogs, and relaxing in the farmhouse's makeshift lounge room. The idea of finding time to read the Bible and engage with their Christian faith came up in conversation with Simon when I asked him about the differences between farm work in Myanmar and in Malaysia. "Here we can rent machines, in Chin State it is all manual labor," he exclaimed and went on, "Here I can read the Bible in the morning and then do some work on the field." Thus, in Malaysia, less work or less manual work means more time for studying his religion, another freedom for which many people specifically fled Chin State. Thus, the aforementioned rhizomatic being can grow and blossom on these farms as refugees discuss, enact, and maintain their religious identity, culture, and practices. Christian religiosity, however, is part of the everyday, and Chin refugees invoked this alter-sovereign continually to make sense of their lives, both past and future. During an immigration raid in Kuala Lumpur, Simon told me, police stopped him, and he prayed to God, hoping for a speedy escape. He offered the officer some money he had on him, and they let him go, sparing him detention and jail: "Every time I pray—God helps me." This belief is a steadfast accompaniment to his everyday life and to his greater hopes and dreams for the future.

THE CAMERON HIGHLANDS: LABOR WITHOUT BELONGING

On another fieldwork trip, I visited a Chin community in the Cameron Highlands, several hours north of Kuala Lumpur. Here, in the cooler environment, most vegetables for the wet markets around the Klang Valley are produced alongside a major tea estate and strawberry farms. As I was chatting to my Chin friend on a small side road, an old Land Cruiser pulled up next to us. It was the type that harks back to British colonial times, when the Cameron Highlands served as a hill station and summer retreat. Now, they seem primarily used to ferry back and forth produce from the market gardens and farms scattered across the highlands. Around 3,000 Chin refugees are rumored to live here, and about 2,000 of them have organized into a Highland Chin Community, sponsored by the UNHCR. The community facilities have a computer room, meeting space, and office space. The services are sparse, and few resources are available, but with a system similar to those of other Chin refugee organizations in the city, they are raising funds through registration and the issuance of identity cards. On the first farm we visited that day, we were met by the burly overseer, a Chin man, who had earned the trust of the Orang Asli policeman who owns the farm. Now he was in charge of the four workers who maintained the gardens growing beans and parsley on a steep hill in the highlands.

The living arrangements on all the farms we visited were makeshift and very basic. One of the Chin refugees led us to their dormitory, a basic wooden structure with a range of sectioned-off rooms. Some are used by families with makeshift partitions creating bedrooms and separate kitchen areas, while others contain mattresses for up to ten single men arranged side-by-side on bare floors. Yet within this basic infrastructure, entrepreneurial adaptation flourished. Some families had managed to cultivate small gardens behind the dormitory block, growing their own vegetables for cooking that supplemented their wages and reconnected them with agricultural practices from their homelands. The carefully tended plots with rows of chili, bok choy, and herbs represented more than local food security. They embodied continuity with their previous lives, demonstrating how refugees can transform even the most basic and marginal spaces into sites of familiarity and sustenance. At another farm, down a steep road, unregistered refugees revealed the extent of their fear when they showed us their sleeping quarters. They had cut a secret path through dense rainforest to a basic wooden structure serving as a meeting room and lounge. A short uphill walk led to even thicker forest where they had constructed makeshift treehouses hidden in the canopy, invisible from below. The dwellings jutted precariously over ravines, offering minimal shelter. Michael, one of the farm workers who, like many Chin, had adopted a Christian name following American missionary influence, explained they slept in the trees to evade detection during raids. The elevation provided both concealment and advance warning if authorities approached, though the unstable construction meant every night risked a dangerous fall.

Next door, new seeds were planted along with a layer of new topsoil. Landslides and poor soil mean that the majority of farms here transport in topsoil and pesticides to increase yields. Most workers live on the same patch of farm they work on. Here, five workers shared a makeshift tin-roof shack that consisted of a shed for tools and pesticides, a kitchen/diner (a grander term than the picture before me), and a sleeping quarter. There are no windows inside the shack, just darkness and the dreariness of poverty. Working hours are from 7:30 a.m. to 7:30 p.m. every day, with one day off a month. This leaves little time to spend any money they earn, and means most refugees can save more living in the Cameron Highlands than in the city. Even so, they only receive RM 800–900 (USD 200) a month for their work. But the remoteness and long working hours mean they rarely leave the farm.

Families find living here gives them more security than in Kuala Lumpur, as well as more money in the end. However, the trade-off is that there are fewer education opportunities and health services: a Christian NGO runs a bimonthly mobile health clinic here, and a small school just started, with one teacher and nine students who stay at the school during the week. As we left for the day, we passed a bunch of motorbikes on the side of the street. In the distance, we could see men playing football. I was told it was Orang Asli and Chin playing together: "They have become friends here."

FINDING NEW WAYS OF DWELLING

Throughout this book, I chronicle a range of techniques that allow places and lives to exist, even if temporarily, outside the state's purview. Farming and kinship/family have been potent symbolic resources as well as practices that allow for affective repertoires beyond survival, and beyond refugees as contained objectification, such as cheap labor, illegal immigrant, or radical other. Thus, refugees on the farms escape some of these objectifying techniques invoked by the Malaysian state, the economy, and a racialized Malaysian society. The activities described in this chapter point toward ways refugees have made and are actively engaged in making the farms their homes, attaching meaning and an affective relationship to place, and developing a sense of belonging to their farms. The planting, working on, and manipulation of the land create a deep-seated attachment to a specific patch of land. In the case of Simon and Mary in Batu Arang, the refugee farm has inherited spatial markers, such as the fence that encloses the farm, but Simon negotiated access to another farm to fish and hunt, and began bartering between some of the refugee farms. Thus, his activities extend beyond "his farm" into a shared gift economy where commodities are traded, access and surplus are exchanged, and time and expertise are offered to one another whenever possible. These activities point to a series of alternative ways of being a refugee. Thus, I take up Ghassan Hage's (2012) anthropological mission to uncover and find what he calls "minor realities," spaces outside-domestication, that engage otherness on its own terms; in short, to find spaces and people who live and engage in alter-politics. And it is here that rhizomatic identity pierces the surface, and a minor reality of dwelling comes to fruition.

In comparison to the large numbers of refugees living in urban environments, what I describe here is on a very small scale and not a realistic alternative for all refugees living in Malaysia. However, their mere existence and ability to create the farms as a minor reality are significant in themselves. Here, refugees can be seen not just as resisting specific attempts at containment and world-making around them, but also as inhabitants of places of their own making. The Malaysian state, the UNHCR, the economy, and global networks persist alongside and within refugees' conceptions of self and the world they are making for themselves on these farms. These worlds represent something different from their previous lives and are marked by multiplicity and aleatory effects and affects that allow some refugees to inhabit them and bring about new ones. The agricultural dimension of refugee place-making demonstrates how displaced populations can create meaningful alternatives to urban survival strategies while simultaneously challenging dominant assumptions about citizenship, belonging, and the relationship between people and land. Through their farming activities, refugees like Simon and Mary develop forms of agency that operate beyond the constraints of legal exclusion, creating spaces of belonging that draw on homeland practices while adapting to Malaysian conditions, a theme I take up in the next chapter through the domains of sport and national day celebrations.

CHAPTER 7

Making Community and Nation through Sport and Cultural Celebration

On a humid afternoon in Ampang, in the north of Kuala Lumpur, I stand pitchside watching two teams take to a government school field. Ampang FC, wearing knock-off FC Barcelona jerseys purchased from shops around Kuala Lumpur, faces the Rohingya Football Club (RFC), whose players wear distinctive jerseys bearing Rohingya symbols and colors. Around the field, 50–60 mostly Rohingya onlookers gather, some waving flags, some engrossed in conversation, their voices mingling with the commentary from loudspeakers, as local Malaysian residents watch curiously from their backyard fences.

This scene, repeated across various fields throughout Kuala Lumpur, represents far more than recreational sport, as it also embodies a complex process of identity maintenance, community building, and strategic visibility within Malaysian society.

For refugees living in legal limbo in Malaysia, sporting and cultural activities serve as crucial mechanisms for transcending mere survival and engaging in meaningful community building. Following Brun's (2001) call to "reterritorialize" the relationship between people and place in refugee studies, this chapter examines how sporting and cultural activities, such as football and national day celebrations, enable refugees to forge new territorial relationships that challenge the deterritorializing effects of displacement and systematic exclusion.

Through an ethnographic analysis of the RFC and Chin and Zomi national day celebrations, this chapter demonstrates how sporting and cultural practices enable refugees to maintain their identities while building social capital within and across communities. Drawing on Çağlar and Glick Schiller's (2018) concept of "sociabilities of emplacement," I argue that these activities function as place-making practices that enable refugees to create spaces of belonging and security within often hostile environments. The sporting and cultural activities examined here represent forms of "strategic visibility" for refugees, i.e., calculated decisions to assert presence in public spaces despite the risks such visibility entails. I begin with an exploration of sports in refugee contexts, then engage with the RFC case study and, subsequently, the national day celebrations.

FIGURE 17 Rohingya community members gathering to watch RFC matches

SPORT AND REFUGEE INTEGRATION: CRITICAL PERSPECTIVES

Research from refugee resettlement countries such as Denmark, Norway, and Australia provides crucial insights into how sporting activities function in refugee integration processes, though these findings must be carefully contextualized when applied to non-signatory and transit countries such as Malaysia. The integration literature shows tensions between policy intentions and lived experiences, echoing what Schinkel (2013) identified as the "problematic of integration." Integration discourses typically place responsibility on newcomers to adapt to existing social norms while providing inadequate support for such adaptation, and this dynamic is intensified in Malaysia, where no integration policies exist.

In Denmark, sports clubs have become "arenas for ethnic integration," ascribed a central role in "distributing social capital, promoting equality in society and facilitating informal learning" (Agergaard 2011, 350). However, Agergaard's ethnographic analysis reveals significant gaps between policy intentions and lived experiences. As Agergaard and Michelsen la Cour (2012) observe, the expectation that "cultural adaptation of ethnic minorities to Danish values and norms can be fostered by civil society actors such as sports organizations" assumes a degree of cultural homogeneity that does not exist in practice. Their research reveals how "civil integration and cultural assimilation" operate as "different priorities" that may conflict with the "ideas, values and aims of organizations and their projects" (28).

The Danish experience also demonstrates how sporting activities can reproduce rather than challenge social hierarchies. Agergaard and Sørensen's (2009) analysis of ethnic minority football players shows that physical capital must be combined with cultural and social capital to achieve social mobility. Crucially, outcomes differ across suburbs and socioeconomic milieus, suggesting that sporting excellence alone cannot overcome structural inequalities, as will become evident in the Malaysian context, where class and gender exclusions shape participation in refugee sporting activities.

The concept of social capital provides a crucial analytical framework for understanding how sporting activities function in refugee communities, though its application requires careful attention to power relations and structural inequalities. Walseth's (2008) Norwegian study makes an important analytical distinction between "bridging social capital" (between different ethnic groups) and "bonding social capital" (maintaining existing relationships with people similar to oneself). Her ethnographic research with young Muslim women reveals that while sports clubs might serve as arenas for bridging social capital among immigrants across ethnicities, they play a more limited role in bridging social capital "across social class and the immigrant-non-immigrant divide" (15).

This finding resonates with broader critiques of social capital theory that emphasize its tendency to individualize structural problems. As Anthias (2007) argues, social capital discourse often places responsibility on marginalized communities to "build bridges" while ignoring the structural barriers that prevent such bridge-building. In the Malaysian context, where refugees face systematic exclusion from formal employment, education, and healthcare, the limitations of social capital approaches become particularly pronounced.

Ramon Spaaij's extensive research with Somali refugees in Melbourne shows how sporting activities, especially organized sport, function to rebuild social relationships disrupted by displacement (2011, 86). Significantly, for Somali refugees in Melbourne, "social encounters in sport are important [...] arguably even more important than the sports activity itself" (86). His research further shows that "bonding in the sports context has overcome some of the clan-based cleavages which were endemic in Somalia," suggesting that sporting activities can serve as powerful mechanisms for community cohesion even across traditional social divisions (87). However, he also notes that "sport's contribution to social capital should however be neither overstated nor over-generalized. Bridging social capital in sport is relatively weak and few bridges are established between Somalis and the host community" (Spaaij 2012, 1519). Indeed, discrimination, prejudice, and generally negative encounters between communities can harden the boundaries between social groups when the only place they meet is in an oppositional game of football.

THE MALAYSIAN CONTEXT

Malaysia presents a unique context for understanding the role of sport in refugee communities, one that challenges many assumptions derived from resettlement-country research. The sporting and cultural activities examined here demonstrate what Isin (2008) terms "acts of citizenship," practices that claim rights and recognition without waiting for formal legal acknowledgment, i.e., to simply create the conditions for their existence in Malaysian society. There is limited Malaysian literature on sport and inclusion, and even less on refugees. Baidruel Hairiel Abd Rahim and Nurazzura Mohamad Diah's (2012) study of minority students in sports-based character school programs suggests that sports can serve as a tool for integration and social control in multicultural settings such as Malaysia. However, their research reveals the assimilatory assumptions underlying such programs, which require minority students to embrace the Malaysian educational system. For refugees in Malaysia, participating in sporting activities requires navigating not only these cultural preferences but also significant structural constraints. Ramalingam's (2011) work on sport as a "solution for multiculturalism" further depicts the gap between official rhetoric and lived experience. While the government promotes sport as a mechanism for fostering "unity and equality," refugees remain systematically excluded from formal sporting institutions and must create their own alternative spaces for cultural expression.

Religion shapes how these activities unfold and how Malaysian society receives them. Malaysia's designation as a Muslim-majority state creates opportunities and constraints for different refugee communities. While Islamic NGOs and individual Muslims have provided support to refugee communities, this support operates within ethnic and sectarian boundaries that limit broader integration (Hoffstaedter 2017b). This can provide specific forms of recognition for Muslim refugees unavailable to non-Muslim communities. However, even Muslim refugees face significant barriers, as religious solidarity cannot overcome racial and ethnic prejudices. These boundaries shape how sporting activities are received. The positive response to the RFC's tournament with Malaysian corporate teams reflects both football's appeal as a universal language and the Islamic identity of many team members. The following analysis of the RFC demonstrates how these theoretical insights play out in practice, revealing both the possibilities and limitations of sporting activities as mechanisms for community building, identity maintenance, and strategic visibility within conditions of structural marginality.

CREATING A NATIONAL TEAM IN EXILE: THE ROHINGYA FOOTBALL CLUB

The RFC emerged in 2015 as, in its organizers' description, a "national team in exile." Unlike neighborhood teams such as Ampang FC, which draws players from specific residential areas, the RFC recruits the best players from across Kuala Lumpur and beyond. This organizational structure reflects deep aspirations for national representation and recognition. As a stateless people, the Rohingya have been denied not only citizenship but the basic markers of national identity that most communities take for granted. The creation of the RFC thus represents an attempt to establish forms of national representation and sovereignty within the constraints of exile and displacement.

FIGURE 18 Old and new RFC flags displayed at matches, a symbol of national identity in exile

The club's visual identity makes these aspirations unmistakable. While Ampang FC wears readily available Barcelona jerseys, the RFC has invested in distinctive jerseys and flags that prominently display Rohingya symbols and colors. Some flags are hand-painted by supporters, others professionally printed. Their importance cannot be overstated, as they represent identity and being part of a Rohingya diaspora that has not forgotten its roots. Supporters often attend games carrying these flags, planting them around the field, transforming ordinary football pitches into temporary homelands. In 2015, the Kick-Project, an Australian NGO I supported, was awarded a grant from the Australian High Commission in Malaysia to help the RFC purchase new jerseys, cover transportation costs, and rent training grounds for team practices and games. We worked together to establish the club's operations and its many forays in establishing itself as a diaspora team for the Rohingya community.

FIGURE 19 Team announcements at an RFC match

The RFC's activities have created what Bey (1991) conceptualized as "temporary autonomous zones," or spaces where alternative forms of social organization can emerge outside state control. Following Ong's (2006) work on "graduated sovereignty," these sporting activities create spaces where different forms of sovereignty overlap and, from the bottom up, create forms of self-organization and representation. The placement of flags, the use of loudspeakers, and the gathering of supporters all serve to territorialize space, challenging dominant assumptions about who has the right to occupy public spaces in Malaysia.

The strategic nature of this visibility becomes apparent in the RFC's choice to play in plain view of the local community and passing traffic while maintaining distinctive visual markers of Rohingya identity. This represents a calculated decision to assert presence in public spaces despite the risks. For Rohingya refugees, whose homeland remains inaccessible due to ongoing persecution, the football field becomes a space where forms of national identity and belonging can be performed and maintained. The flags and jerseys serve as material reminders and stakeholders that help maintain cultural identity across spatial and temporal displacement. The RFC's activities transform ordinary football fields into sites of cultural assertion, and one can even argue that they constitute political claim-making. However, these zones also reveal limitations and vulnerabilities. The temporary nature of these autonomous spaces reflects the precarious position of refugee communities in Malaysia, where official tolerance can be withdrawn at any moment. The need to negotiate access to playing fields, coordinate with local authorities, and maintain relationships with Malaysian communities all demonstrate the conditional nature of refugee agency in these contexts.

In 2016, the RFC organized a tournament with Malaysian corporate teams. It was a major success as it was the first time a Rohingya team played Malaysian teams. The corporate teams of Astro Awani, a major media organization; Tenaga Nasional, a major utility company; and Utusan Malaysia, a major Malay-language newspaper, all participated and played several games at Tenaga Nasional's stadium in Kuala Lumpur. It was a one-off, but with media companies' attendance and involvement, it received strong media attention, with journalists attending and covering the event. The young Rohingya team dominated the mostly middle-aged corporate teams and I remember telling the RFC captain that it may be good to let the other team score the odd goal to allow them to feel included, but to the team, winning and scoring high was part of the appeal to demonstrate that they were good and to be recognized for their football prowess, not always reduced to their outsider refugee status. Thus, they annihilated every other team that day, invoking chants of "Allahu akbar"—God is the greatest—and proudly flying their flags. Later that year, they officially entered a Malaysian social football league.

FIGURE 20 Teams from Malaysian corporate teams and the RFC competing in a friendly football tournament

The club's success in attracting positive media attention and building relationships with Malaysian teams demonstrates the potential effectiveness of strategic visibility through sports. Such an approach is less confronting than making outright political claims and allows for tensions to be worked through within a set of rules. This strategic visibility also functions as what Butler (2015) calls "performative assembly," i.e., the ways marginalized groups claim political recognition through collective public appearance. Butler's analysis of how "bodies in alliance" can challenge dominant power structures can help us understand how refugee sporting activities can function as political performances even when they appear purely recreational.

The tournament created opportunities for contact with Malaysians whom Rohingya refugees would otherwise never meet; however, football games are short, and afterward, there is usually no time or space to talk across team lines. It was striking that, even at the social football event with corporate teams, where such time was afforded, no supporters or spectators had been invited. The games were played to an empty stadium, partly because the presence of refugees—"undocumented people" in the eyes of

Malaysian authorities—was not something major corporations in Malaysia wanted to advertise. The positive media coverage and public reception after the event indicated some success in challenging negative stereotypes, but the sustainability of these gains remains questionable given broader patterns of conditional hospitality in Malaysian society.

The bonding social capital function of the RFC serves particularly crucial functions, given the dispersed nature of Rohingya settlement in Kuala Lumpur. The club's role as a diaspora national team in exile creates connections that transcend neighborhood boundaries and workplace relationships, providing what Putnam (2000) terms "social glue" that holds communities together. However, this bonding function also creates potential exclusions. The emphasis on recruiting the "best players" may marginalize less skilled community members, reflecting broader patterns of inequality within refugee communities that sporting activities may reproduce rather than challenge.

A couple of years ago, the RFC became an official member of the Confederation of Independent Football Associations (CONIFA), an international football organization for teams from stateless peoples, minorities, and unrecognized states, which provides a form of international recognition that operates entirely outside Malaysian state structures. It also reinforced the RFC's role as a focal point for the Rohingya diaspora and its representational power to be the "national team in exile."

Much of the work with the RFC was very positive and led to material changes for Rohingya refugees, but the gendered dimensions of the RFC's activities became a significant limitation. During my fieldwork, we attempted to include women and establish a women's football section, but this remained a mere hope, with efforts mired in discussions and false starts. Some women were interested in playing, and at times there was an upswing in interest, especially among young women. However, the gender politics of Rohingya patriarchal society was mirrored in the RFC, its leadership, and their priorities. Many male players saw the involvement of women not only as culturally problematic but as direct competition for their resources. The overwhelmingly male participation in both playing and supporting roles reflects broader patterns of gender exclusion in Rohingya refugee communities as well as other refugee groups. Drawing on Spaaij's (2015) analysis of gender boundaries in refugee sport, this pattern suggests that sporting activities may reinforce rather than challenge patriarchal structures within refugee communities. However, Palmer's (2009) research on soccer and the politics of identity for young Muslim refugee women provides a useful counterpoint. Her analysis demonstrates how sporting activities can provide spaces for women to negotiate between Islamic traditions and Western popular culture, but also shows the uphill battles and support structures needed to overcome the significant constraints that limit women's participation in public sporting activities.

Despite its successes, the RFC faces significant challenges that reflect broader structural constraints facing refugee communities in Malaysia. The precarious legal status of participants creates a constant risk of arrest and detention, limiting the club's capacity for development and expansion. The lack of formal recognition means that facilities and equipment must be secured through informal arrangements. The absence of official support and secure funding sources means that activities depend on voluntary contributions from community members who themselves face economic insecurity.

CELEBRATING DIFFERENCE: CHIN AND ZOMI NATIONAL DAY CELEBRATIONS

The annual Chin and Zomi national day celebrations in Kuala Lumpur represent another crucial example of how refugees use cultural practices to maintain identity and build community. These celebrations, held in venues such as the central Chin Woo Stadium overlooking Kuala Lumpur's Chinatown or the Kuala Lumpur & Selangor Chinese Assembly Hall just down the road, bring together several hundred refugees from Myanmar in public displays of cultural identity and national aspiration.

Chin Woo Stadium, once the place where Malaysian athletes trained, is owned by the Selangor Chinese Athletic Association and has been a Kuala Lumpur landmark for over 60 years. On this day in February, the hall is filled with an excited crowd of several hundred refugees from Myanmar. They are celebrating their (ethnic) national day in diaspora. The significance of these celebrations cannot be understood without considering the risks involved. Given the constant threats of police extortion and immigration raids, it is highly irregular for refugees to venture out to meet and congregate in such a public place. The continuance of these celebrations despite these risks demonstrates their fundamental importance to community well-being and identity maintenance.

The celebrations themselves follow established patterns of national commemoration: traditional dress, songs, prayers, speeches, and communal gathering. In the foyer, Zomi women sell food, traditional scarves, and children's clothes. Women and men both participate visibly, with traditional dress and cultural performances providing opportunities for women's participation beyond what is available in sporting activities. These elements serve to maintain what Benedict Anderson (1983) termed an "imagined community," a sense of shared identity and belonging that transcends immediate geographical or social boundaries. For refugees living in legal limbo, these celebrations provide important opportunities to affirm their cultural identity and maintain connections to their traditions and homeland.

FIGURE 21 Chin refugees celebrating ethnic diversity during National Day events

The separate Chin and Zomi national day celebrations reflect complex transnational identity politics that extend far beyond the Malaysian context. The creation of a so-called Chin ethnic, or even national, identity was a product of British colonialism and of Chin leaders following Burma's independence, while a pan-regional Zo-identity (*zo-mi* means "hill people") has reasserted itself, claiming a much larger political and cultural space. These celebrations thus represent more than simple cultural maintenance; they constitute active participation in ongoing debates about political and cultural identity that span multiple nation-states. The refugees have transplanted the debate over their political and cultural future into a transnational space that stretches from Myanmar to Malaysia and beyond to their resettlement countries.

FIGURE 22 Chin National Day celebrations include a range of activities

This transnational dimension demonstrates how refugee communities in Malaysia are not simply passive recipients of circumstances but active participants in broader political and cultural movements. The celebrations serve as sites where competing visions of identity and belonging are negotiated and affirmed, contributing to ongoing processes of nation-building and cultural definition that extend across national boundaries.

FIGURE 23 Zomi National Day celebrations maintaining cultural traditions and homeland connections

Community identity and the roles culture and religion play in this are crucial to building and maintaining resilience in the face of legal, political, and social deprivation. The celebrations provide opportunities for refugees to experience recognition and validation that is largely absent from their daily lives, lives characterized by legal precarity and social marginalization.

The celebratory context also enables forms of social interaction and community building that might otherwise be impossible given spatial restrictions and enforcement patterns. The gathering of several hundred refugees in public spaces creates opportunities for networking, information sharing, and mutual support that extend far beyond the event itself. These connections contribute to the social capital that enables refugee communities to survive and thrive despite structural constraints. The stadium had supplied security staff to keep the peace at this large National Day gathering, who (ironically) happened to be officers from the People's Volunteer Corps (*Jabatan Sukarelawan Malaysia*, or RELA). In the refugee community, RELA officers are feared as they are often used as auxiliary police by the immigration department for raids. RELA had a reputation for being violent and mean; often, refugees would recount how RELA officers had thrown away their UNHCR card or roughed them up during a raid. This reputation was the consequence of poor training and the inducements that authorities paid RELA officers for catching undocumented people. Many RELA officers took it for granted that they had police powers, which they wielded indiscriminately, ultimately causing the government to step in 15 years ago and largely remove them from enforcement activities. At the national day celebration, their army fatigues and yellow berets raised some concern among attendees, but the RELA officers who took on the new security role for the event smiled and opened doors for attendees.

FIGURE 24 Wares for sale during the Zomi National Day celebration, a RELA officer in the background

The Chin/Zomi celebrations also reveal significant challenges and contradictions within refugee communities. The separate celebrations of closely related ethnic groups demonstrate how cultural maintenance can sometimes reinforce divisions rather than promote unity, divisions that reflect complex identity politics and colonial legacies.

The public nature of these celebrations also creates tension between visibility and security. While the celebrations assert cultural identity and demand recognition, they also expose participants to potential risks from authorities and hostile community members. The decision to continue celebrating despite these risks reflects the fundamental importance of cultural identity to community well-being, but also highlights the difficult choices refugee communities must make between safety and self-expression.

THE PARADOX OF VISIBILITY

Both the RFC and the Chin/Zomi national day celebrations demonstrate a paradox of visibility that challenges conventional understandings of refugee behavior. Rather than seeking invisibility as a survival strategy, these communities actively assert their presence in Malaysian public spaces. This strategic visibility serves multiple functions: challenging stereotypes, creating opportunities for interaction, and asserting cultural identity despite legal marginalization.

The success of this strategy depends partly on the non-threatening nature of sporting and cultural activities. These activities can present refugee communities in positive, non-political contexts that may be more acceptable to Malaysian society than other forms of public assertion. The emphasis on skill, organization, and cultural richness provides alternative narratives to dominant discourses that frame refugees primarily as problems or burdens.

However, the strategy of visibility also creates vulnerabilities. Public gatherings create opportunities for harassment, arrest, and deportation. The strategic calculation to remain visible despite these risks suggests that the benefits of cultural assertion and community building outweigh the potential costs, reflecting the fundamental importance of identity and belonging to human well-being.

BUILDING COMMUNITY THROUGH TEMPORARY SOVEREIGNTY

Both RFC matches and national day celebrations create temporary spaces where refugees exercise forms of sovereignty by making decisions about organization, representation, and cultural expression without external control, control that is otherwise pervasive in their daily lives. These zones serve multiple functions beyond their immediate purposes. They provide opportunities for community members to exercise leadership and organizational skills that are largely unused in other contexts. They create spaces where alternative forms of authority and legitimacy can be recognized and validated. They also serve as sites where community members can experience the dignity and recognition that are largely absent from their daily lives.

The temporary nature of these zones reflects the structural constraints facing refugee communities, but it also demonstrates the creativity and resilience with which communities adapt to difficult circumstances. The ability to create meaningful spaces of self-determination, even temporarily, provides crucial resources for community well-being and identity maintenance.

The activities examined in this chapter demonstrate how refugee communities engage in practices of cultural citizenship that transcend legal recognition (Rosaldo 1997). Through sporting activities and cultural celebrations, refugees assert their right to belong to Malaysian society while maintaining their distinct cultural identities. The concept of cultural citizenship is particularly relevant in the Malaysian context, where formal pathways to integration are largely absent. However, the limitations of cultural citizenship also become apparent through these case studies. While sporting activities and cultural celebrations provide important opportunities for community building and identity maintenance, they do not address fundamental structural inequalities and vulnerabilities that affect refugee communities. The persistence of discrimination, exploitation, and legal marginalization despite successful community activities highlights the need for more comprehensive approaches to refugee integration.

SOCIAL CAPITAL: BONDING, BRIDGING, AND LINKING

Both case studies demonstrate the crucial role of sporting and cultural activities in building social capital within refugee communities. The RFC brings together Rohingya refugees from across Kuala Lumpur, creating connections that transcend neighborhood boundaries. The national day celebrations similarly unite community members who might otherwise remain isolated in their respective residential areas, where they face spatial restrictions and mobility constraints.

This bonding social capital serves multiple practical functions. It provides information networks that help community members navigate bureaucratic challenges, find employment, and access services that are largely denied through formal channels. It creates support networks that provide assistance during crises and emergencies, complementing existing mutual aid systems. It also maintains cultural knowledge and practices that might otherwise be lost in the diaspora context. The strength of bonding social capital within refugee communities reflects both the challenges they face and the resources they possess. The shared experience of displacement, marginalization, and legal vulnerability creates strong incentives for mutual support and cooperation.

The development of bridging social capital, or the connections across ethnic and cultural boundaries, proves more challenging but not impossible. The RFC's interactions with Malaysian teams and communities demonstrate that sports can foster cross-cultural understanding and cooperation. The tournament with Malaysian company teams, while limited in scope, provided a model for how such interactions might be expanded, though within the constraints of ethnic and religious boundaries.

The limitations of bridging social capital are also apparent in both case studies. The limited participation of Malaysians in both football games, or in refugee national cultural celebrations, and the persistence of discrimination despite positive interactions all suggest that structural barriers to integration remain significant. However, even limited bridging social capital should not be dismissed. The conversations between RFC supporters and Malaysian neighbors, the media coverage of community activities, and the participation of refugee teams in Malaysian tournaments all represent forms of social connection that transcend ethnic boundaries. These connections, while limited, provide foundations for expanded interaction and understanding.

The development of linking social capital, i.e., the connections to formal institutions and power structures, remains the most constrained aspect of refugee community activities. The absence of formal recognition for refugee communities in Malaysia limits opportunities for institutional connections and support. However, both case studies demonstrate some success in developing alternative forms of linking social capital that operate outside formal state structures.

The RFC's membership in CONIFA provides formal recognition and legitimacy within alternative football structures. This international recognition, while outside the official national football organization, provides a form of validation that extends beyond the Malaysian context. The media coverage of community activities also creates connections to public discourse and debate that might otherwise be absent, and that discourse can challenge exclusionary narratives. The national day celebrations demonstrate another form of linking social capital through their connections to transnational political movements and cultural networks—from their homelands via Malaysia to the wider diaspora (especially in resettlement countries). The ability to participate in ongoing debates about identity and belonging across national boundaries provides a form of political engagement that transcends local limitations.

CONCLUSION: BEYOND SURVIVAL, TOWARD COMMUNITY

Through the RFC and the Chin/Zomi national day celebrations, refugee communities engage in the active process of creating meaningful presence and belonging in places of displacement. These activities challenge dominant theoretical frameworks that position refugees as passive victims of circumstances beyond their control. Instead, they reveal what Çağlar and Glick Schiller (2018) identify as "migrants' city-making practices," the ways mobile populations actively contribute to urban social life despite their formal exclusion from rights. The temporary autonomous zones created through sporting and cultural activities represent exercises in "insurgent citizenship," or the claiming of rights and recognition through practice rather than formal legal procedures (Holston 1999).

However, the analysis also reveals significant limitations that reflect broader structural inequalities affecting refugee communities in Malaysia. The gendered dimensions of sporting participation and the conditional nature of Malaysian acceptance demonstrate that cultural recognition cannot substitute for structural inclusion. As Hage (1998) argues in his analysis of Australian multiculturalism, cultural celebration can serve to mask rather than address underlying relations of domination and exclusion.

The experiences of refugee communities in Malaysia demonstrate that integration is not simply a matter of policy implementation but a complex process of negotiation, adaptation, and creativity that involves both refugee communities and host societies. The sporting activities and cultural celebrations examined here represent just one aspect of this broader process, but they provide crucial insights into how communities maintain identity and build belonging in circumstances that might otherwise appear to offer little hope for meaningful participation or recognition.

The temporary autonomous zones created through sporting activities and cultural celebrations may be fleeting, but their significance extends far beyond their duration. They represent exercises in possibility, demonstrations of capacity, and assertions of dignity that challenge dominant narratives about refugee communities while building foundations for alternative forms of belonging and participation. In an era of increasing global displacement and mobility, understanding these processes becomes crucial for developing more inclusive and responsive approaches to integration and social cohesion.

CONCLUSION

Being, Living, Emplacing, and Being Some More

On a sweltering afternoon in Batu Arang, Simon tends to his injured monkey while Mary prepares betel leaves for the city market. Fifty kilometers away in Kuala Lumpur, members of the Rohingya Football Club unfurl their hand-painted flags on a football field, preparing for another match that asserts their presence in Malaysian public space. These seemingly disparate scenes, ranging from agricultural emplacement to national cultural celebration, represent different parts within a wide spectrum of refugee place-making in contemporary Malaysia. They embody the movement from mere survival toward meaningful emplacement, a journey that challenges conventional understandings of refugee agency, urban citizenship, and the possibilities for belonging within exclusionary state systems.

This study demonstrates how Chin and Rohingya refugees navigate polycrisis conditions characterized by intersecting legal exclusion, economic marginalization, health vulnerabilities, and social discrimination. Rather than documenting suffering or celebrating resilience, it reveals how refugees actively create spaces of belonging and self-determination despite systematic attempts to reduce them to what Agamben (1998) terms "bare life." The central finding challenges dominant narratives: refugees in Malaysia do not merely survive within hostile environments; they create alternative forms of social organization, economic participation, and cultural expression that fundamentally question assumptions about citizenship, belonging, and the nation-state itself.

The journey through bureaucratic recognition, daily urban survival, and diverse place-making practices exposes refugee experiences that defy simple categorization. The examination of "becoming" a refugee in chapter 3 shows how UNHCR registration creates certain forms of subjectivity requiring refugees to perform victimhood or present an essentialized identity while navigating corruption, delays, and community gatekeeping. Yet refugees exercise agency through strategic storytelling, document management, and community organizing that transcends individual survival to encompass collective empowerment.

Urban survival strategies in chapter 5 demonstrate how refugees navigate legal precarity. From police encounters requiring split-second decisions about visibility and documentation, to healthcare systems serving as surveillance sites rather than sanctuaries, refugees develop "strategic visibility," i.e., calculated decisions about when to assert presence and when to remain invisible. The invisible support networks they create provide not merely material assistance but emotional sustenance and cultural continuity, enabling community flourishing despite systematic exclusion.

Agricultural life, as explained in chapter 6, extends place-making beyond urban contexts to rural alternatives, challenging territorial assumptions about belonging. Farming communities in Batu Arang create spaces where refugees experience a degree of freedom and dignity largely absent from city life, and develop economic activities that operate largely outside state surveillance. These experiments tell us about the profound human need for connection to the land and how displaced populations adapt traditional practices to ever-new circumstances.

Sporting activities and cultural celebrations in chapter 7 represent the most visible forms of refugee place-making, forming spaces that resemble Bey's "temporary autonomous zones," in which alternative forms of sovereignty and self-determination can take root. The Rohingya Football Club and Chin/Zomi National Day celebrations demonstrate how cultural practices enable refugees to maintain identity while building social capital across ethnic and religious boundaries, revealing both the possibilities and limitations of strategic visibility within conditional hospitality frameworks.

THE POLYCRISIS FRAMEWORK, OTHERING, AND ALTERNATIVE POLITICS

The polycrisis framework provides a more nuanced understanding of how multiple intersecting crises create effects exceeding the sum of their parts. Unlike approaches that isolate legal, economic, or social challenges, this framework shows how health exclusions intensify economic vulnerabilities, legal precarity shapes spatial mobility, and social discrimination affects bureaucratic encounters. The COVID-19 pandemic exemplified these dynamics, revealing how health crises rapidly transform economic integration into social scapegoating.

The framework's theoretical contributions extend beyond refugee studies to broader questions about urban citizenship and social belonging in an era of increasing global mobility. The ongoing legal limbo and resulting precarity allow non-signatory countries like Malaysia to benefit economically from refugee labor while avoiding political responsibilities for protection. Malaysia deploys "strategic ambiguity" through deliberate policies that neither fully include nor completely exclude displaced populations, thus maintaining flexibility to adjust responses to changing political and economic circumstances.

However, the polycrisis framework also risks creating analytical paralysis by emphasizing overwhelming intersecting challenges. Its utility depends on maintaining focus on refugee agency and innovation. The Malaysian case demonstrates that polycrisis conditions, while constraining, create cracks in (state) systems that can generate opportunities for creative adaptation and alternative social organization that might not emerge under more stable circumstances.

Refugees are continually othered, if they are identified as refugees, and in terms of the body politic, they are subject to "radical othering" in that refugees occupy positions outside normal categories of social and political belonging in Malaysia. Unlike other forms of othering that acknowledge the "other" as part of a shared social universe, radical othering places refugees outside the ambit of domestic politics and spheres of belonging. In Malaysia's already intricate system of ethnic categorization of Malay/bumiputera, Chinese, and Indian ethnic groups, refugees exist outside these state-maintained categories.

This positioning serves multiple functions: it creates scapegoats for societal tensions, deflects attention from Malaysia's deep-seated racial and political divisions, and reinforces Malaysian national identity through contrast with the excluded "them." Yet this radical otherness possesses a lingering presence that can also unsettle existing systems of domination (see Baudrillard 1993). Refugees' very existence outside Malaysia's ethnic framework, then, illustrates the contingent and constructed nature of these categories, opening spaces for alternative forms of political belonging.

The conditional hospitality examined throughout this book, ranging from religious networks providing crucial support to their reticence in associating with refugees, demonstrates both the possibilities and limitations of informal integration. While individual acts of kindness provide crucial support, they cannot substitute for strong policy frameworks recognizing refugee rights and contributions. Religious and ethnic networks offer vital assistance that formal humanitarian systems cannot replace, yet these same networks reproduce exclusions and hierarchies limiting accessibility.

Policymakers designing protection frameworks must recognize the myriad survival strategies refugees already employ while addressing the structural barriers that limit the effectiveness of those frameworks in countries that lack legal protection for refugees. The success of refugee community organizations in Malaysia demonstrates potential for community-based approaches that recognize refugee agency while providing institutional support for self-organizing initiatives. The documentation of strategic refugee visibility in these chapters shows us that refugees possess complex understandings of local political dynamics that can inform advocacy and policy engagement. Rather than assuming refugees prefer invisibility, policymakers should explore how refugee communities want to engage with broader society and what forms of recognition would prove most valuable.

Yet cultural recognition cannot substitute for structural inclusion. The persistence of discrimination, exploitation, and legal marginalization despite successful community activities highlights the need for comprehensive approaches addressing both cultural and material dimensions of integration. The gendered and class-based exclusions documented throughout this book demand policy approaches attending to internal diversity within refugee communities rather than treating them as homogeneous populations.

Breaking the current Malaysian "protection paradox," wherein Malaysia provides some economic integration while enforcing refugee social exclusion, requires regional approaches that recognize refugee mobility as normal rather than a crisis to be contained and deterred. Malaysia's non-signatory status has obvious limitations but can provide space for innovative adaptations by refugees and humanitarian actors that could inform more inclusive protection frameworks.

THE PERSISTENCE OF PLACE-MAKING

This conclusion's title captures the ongoing, processual nature of refugee place-making documented throughout. Unlike sedentarist assumptions that equate security with rootedness in a given territory, the refugee experiences examined here reveal forms of belonging that transcend territorial boundaries while creating meaningful connections to specific places. Agricultural life in Batu Arang, sporting activities across Kuala Lumpur, and cultural celebrations across Malaysian cities all demonstrate human creativity in making place, despite exclusionary circumstances.

These place-making practices reveal the hard work required to transform abstract space into meaningful place through social relationships, cultural practices, and emotional investment. For refugees living in legal limbo, this work becomes particularly crucial; with formal citizenship pathways remaining largely blocked, alternative forms of belonging must be created in their stead through daily practice. The temporary autonomous zones created through sporting and cultural activities may be fleeting, but their significance extends far beyond their duration as exercises in possibility and assertions of dignity.

The persistence of place-making despite systematic exclusion demonstrates fundamental human capacities transcending legal categories and structural constraints. The desire for belonging, recognition, and self-determination cannot be suppressed by legal marginalization or social exclusion. Instead, these desires find expression through daily or extraordinary practices that challenge dominant assumptions about citizenship while creating alternative forms of social organization.

The refugee experiences documented here offer insights that extend beyond Malaysia to broader questions about social inclusion, urban citizenship, and belonging in an era of increasing global mobility. As cities worldwide face growing numbers of displaced populations from conflict, environmental change, or economic disruption, understanding these place-making strategies becomes indispensable for developing more inclusive and humane responses and integration road maps.

The Malaysian case reveals both possibilities and limitations of informal integration approaches operating outside formal policy frameworks. While refugees demonstrate remarkable creativity in building meaningful lives despite exclusion, the persistence of vulnerabilities and inequalities demonstrates the need for more systematic approaches to inclusion. The challenge for receiving societies lies in developing frameworks that recognize refugee contributions while addressing structural barriers that limit their full participation.

The polycrisis conditions that characterize contemporary displacement require responses that transcend traditional boundaries between humanitarian assistance, development programming, and urban planning. The innovative survival strategies refugees develop often provide bottom-up models for more sustainable and inclusive forms of urban life, benefiting broader populations.

As this book concludes, Simon and Mary have left the farm in Batu Arang behind and moved back to the city for a better education for their child, while the Rohingya Football Club prepares for its next game. These ongoing activities represent not simply individual survival strategies but collective efforts to create more inclusive forms of belonging that challenge exclusionary assumptions about citizenship and community. Their persistence suggests that the human capacity for place-making transcends even the most systematic attempts at exclusion, offering hope for more inclusive futures, recognizing the contributions of all urban residents regardless of their legal status.

Bibliography

Agamben, Giorgio. 1998. *Homo Sacer: Sovereign Power and Bare Life*. Stanford University Press.

Agergaard, Sine. 2011. "The Cultural Politics of Integration: Danish Sports Clubs as Policy Actors." *International Review for the Sociology of Sport* 46 (3): 338–54.

Agergaard, Sine, and Annette Michelsen la Cour. 2012. "Governing Integration Through Sport: A Case Study of Civil Society Involvement in Welfare Policy." *Nordic Journal of Migration Research* 2 (1): 26–34.

Agergaard, Sine, and Jan Kahr Sørensen. 2009. "The Dream of Social Mobility: Ethnic Minority Players in Danish Football Clubs." *Soccer & Society* 10 (6): 766–80.

Agier, Michel. 2002. "Between War and City: Towards an Urban Anthropology of Refugee Camps." *Ethnography* 3 (3): 317–41.

Agier, Michel. 2011. *Managing the Undesirables: Refugee Camps and Humanitarian Government*. Polity Press.

Al Jazeera. 2014. "101 East: Malaysia's Forgotten Refugees" [now titled "Malaysia's Unwanted"]. Documentary broadcast, November 20. https://www.youtube.com/watch?v=qdV3sj76vnA.

Andaya, Barbara Watson, and Leonard Y. Andaya. 2001. *A History of Malaysia*. 2nd ed. University of Hawai'i Press.

Anderson, Benedict. 1983. *Imagined Communities: Reflections on the Origin and Spread of Nationalism*. Verso.

Anthias, Floya. 2007. "Ethnic Ties: Social Capital and the Question of Mobilisability." *The Sociological Review* 55 (4): 788–805.

Appadurai, Arjun. 1996. *Modernity at Large: Cultural Dimensions of Globalization*. University of Minnesota Press.

Asmady Idris. 2012. "Malaysian Non-Governmental Organizations (NGOs) and Humanitarian Issues in Gaza, Palestine." *Jurnal Antarabangsa Kajian Asia Barat* 4 (1): 49–78.

Azis, Avyanthi. 2014. "Urban Refugees in a Graduated Sovereignty: The Experiences of the Stateless Rohingya in the Klang Valley." *Citizenship Studies* 18 (8): 839–54.

Baidruel Hairiel Abd Rahim and Nurazzura Mohamad Diah. 2012. "Integrating Minority Students Through Sekolah Berwatak (Sports-Based Character School) Programme: A Study of Selected Secondary Schools in the District of Pekan, Pahang." *Proceedings ASEAN University Sports Council International Conference 2012*.

Bakewell, Oliver. 2008. "Research Beyond the Categories: The Importance of Policy Irrelevant Research Into Forced Migration." *Journal of Refugee Studies* 21 (4): 432–53.

Barnett, Michael N., and Martha Finnemore. 2004. *Rules for the World: International Organizations in Global Politics*. Cornell University Press.

Barth, Fredrik. 1969. *Ethnic Groups and Boundaries: The Social Organization of Culture Difference*. Universitets Forlaget.

Baudrillard, Jean. 1993. *The Transparency of Evil: Essays on Extreme Phenomena*. Verso.

Bayly, Christopher, and Tim Harper. 2005. *Forgotten Wars: Freedom and Revolution in Southeast Asia*. Harvard University Press.

Betts, Alexander, and Paul Collier. 2017. *Refuge: Transforming a Broken Refugee System*. Allen Lane.

Bey, Hakim. 1991. *T.A.Z.: The Temporary Autonomous Zone*. Autonomedia. https://voidnetwork.gr/wp-content/uploads/2016/09/T.A.Z-the-temporary-autonomous-zone-by-Hakim-Bey.pdf

Blommaert, Jan. 2009. "Language, Asylum, and the National Order." *Current Anthropology* 50 (4), 415–41.

Brees, Inge. 2010. "Burden or Boon? The Impact of Burmese Refugees on Thailand." *Whitehead Journal of Diplomacy and International Relations* 9 (2): 35–47.

Brown, G. K., L. Chee, and M. R. Thompson. 2004. *Towards a Social Compact for Malaysia: Findings and Recommendations*. University of Malaya Centre for Democracy and Elections.

Brun, Cathrine. 2001. "Reterritorializing the Relationship Between People and Place in Refugee Studies." *Geografiska Annaler: Series B, Human Geography* 83 (1): 15–25.

Butler, Judith. 2015. *Notes Toward a Performative Theory of Assembly*. Harvard University Press.

Çağlar, Ayse, and Nina Glick Schiller. 2018. *Migrants and City-Making: Dispossession, Displacement, and Urban Regeneration*. Duke University Press.

Cameron, Hilary Evans. 2010. "Refugee Status Determinations and the Limits of Memory." *International Journal of Refugee Law* 22 (4): 469–511.

Case, William. 2003. *Politics in Southeast Asia: Democracy or Less*. Curzon Press.

Cheah Boon Kheng. 2002. *Malaysia: The Making of a Nation*. Institute of Southeast Asian Studies.

Chin Human Rights Organization. 2012a. *Threats to Our Existence: Persecution of Ethnic Chin Christians in Burma*. CHRO.

Chin Human Rights Organization. 2012b. *Religious Persecution in Chin State*. CHRO.

Chin Refugee Committee. 2013. *Survey Report on Chin Refugees in Malaysia*. CRC.

Coffey, Guy J. 2003. "The Credibility of Credibility Evidence at the Refugee Review Tribunal." *Sydney Law Review* 25 (1): 79-106.

Cohn, Bernard S. 1996. *Colonialism and Its Forms of Knowledge: The British in India*. Princeton University Press.

Colson, Elizabeth. 1971. *The Social Consequences of Resettlement: The Impact of the Kariba Resettlement upon the Gwembe Tonga*. Manchester University Press.

Commissioner of Law Revision. 2006. *Immigration Act 1953/69*. Malaysia.

Cooley, Alexander, and James Ron. 2002. "The NGO Scramble: Organizational Insecurity and the Political Economy of Transnational Action." *International Security* 27 (1): 5–39.

Crisp, Jeff. 2002. "No Solutions in Sight: The Problem of Protracted Refugee Situations in Africa." Refugee Resettlement Research Project Working Paper No. 75. University of California, San Diego.

Crisp, Jeff. 2004. "The Local Integration and Local Settlement of Refugees: A Conceptual and Historical Analysis." New Issues in Refugee Research Working Paper No. 102. UNHCR.

Crisp, Jeff, Naoko Obi, and Liz Umlas. 2012. "But When Will Our Turn Come? A Review of the Implementation of UNHCR's Urban Refugee

Policy in Malaysia." UNHCR Policy Development and Evaluation Service.

Daniel, E. Valentine, and John Chr Knudsen, eds. 1995. *Mistrusting Refugees*. University of California Press.

Darling, Jonathan. 2016. "Privatising Asylum: Neoliberalisation, Depoliticisation and the Governance of Forced Migration." *Transactions of the Institute of British Geographers* 41 (3): 230–43.

Dawson, Carrie. 2014. "Refugee Hotels: The Discourse of Hospitality and the Rise of Immigration Detention in Canada." *University of Toronto Quarterly* 83 (4): 83–99.

de Haas, Hein. 2008. "The Myth of Invasion: The Inconvenient Realities of African Migration to Europe." *Third World Quarterly* 29 (7): 1305–322.

de Haas, Hein. 2023. *How Migration Really Works: The Facts About the Most Divisive Issue in Politics*. John Murray Press.

Deleuze, Gilles, and Félix Guattari. 1987. *A Thousand Plateaus: Capitalism and Schizophrenia*. Translated by Brian Massumi. University of Minnesota Press.

Derrida, Jacques, and Anne Dufourmantelle. 2000. *Of Hospitality*. Translated by Rachel Bowlby. Stanford University Press.

Dudley, Sandra H. 2010. *Materialising Exile: Material Culture and Embodied Experience among Karenni Refugees in Thailand*. Berghahn Books.

Dunn, Elizabeth Cullen. 2017. *No Path Home: Humanitarian Camps and the Grief of Displacement*. Cornell University Press.

Dunn, Elizabeth Cullen, and Jason Cons. 2013. "Aleatory Sovereignty and the Rule of Sensitive Spaces." *Antipode* 46 (1): 92–109.

Eades, Diana. 2010. *Sociolinguistics and the Legal Process*. Multilingual Matters.

Eastmond, Marita. 2007. "Stories as Lived Experience: Narratives in Forced Migration Research." *Journal of Refugee Studies* 20 (2): 248–64.

Fassin, Didier. 2012. *Humanitarian Reason: A Moral History of the Present*. Translated by Rachel Gomme. University of California Press.

Fassin, Didier, and Estelle d'Halluin. 2005. "The Truth From the Body: Medical Certificates as Ultimate Evidence for Asylum Seekers." *American Anthropologist* 107 (4): 597–608.

Fiddian-Qasmiyeh, Elena, Gil Loescher, Katy Long, and Nando Sigona, eds. 2014. *The Oxford Handbook of Refugee and Forced Migration Studies*. Oxford University Press.

Freeman, John. 2016. "The First Post-Brexit Novel: Mohsin Hamid's *Exit West*; A First Look at the Book's Cover, and a Conversation with John

Freeman." *Literary Hub.* October 6. https://lithub.com/the-first-post-brexit-novel-mohsin-hamids-exit-west/.

Furnivall, J. S. 1948. *Colonial Policy and Practice: A Comparative Study of Burma and Netherlands India.* Cambridge University Press.

Giddens, Anthony. 1991. *Modernity and Self-Identity: Self and Society in the Late Modern Age.* Polity Press.

Giersdorf, Stephan, and Aurel Croissant. 2011. "Civil Society and Competitive Authoritarianism in Malaysia." *Journal of Civil Society* 7 (1): 1–21.

Girard, René. 1986. *The Scapegoat.* Johns Hopkins University Press.

Gittleman, Andrea, and Marissa Brodney. 2013. *Patterns of Anti-Muslim Violence in Burma: A Call for Accountability and Prevention.* Physicians for Human Rights.

Good, Anthony. 2007. *Anthropology and Expertise in the Asylum Courts.* Routledge-Cavendish.

Goodwin-Gill, Guy S., and Jane McAdam. 2007. *The Refugee in International Law.* Oxford University Press.

Grabska, Katarzyna. 2006. "Marginalization in Urban Spaces of the Global South: Urban Refugees in Cairo." *Journal of Refugee Studies* 19 (3): 287–307.

Green, Penny, Thomas MacManus, and Alicia de la Cour Venning. 2015. *Countdown to Annihilation: Genocide in Myanmar.* International State Crime Initiative.

Grundy-Warr, Carl, and Wong, Elaine. 2002. "Sanctuary Under a Plastic Sheet: The Unresolved Problem of Rohingya Refugees." *IBRU Boundary and Security Bulletin* 10 (3): 79–91.

Hage, Ghassan. 1997. "At Home in the Entrails of the West: Multiculturalism, Ethnic Food and Migrant Home-Building." In *Home/world: Space, Community and Marginality in Sydney's West,* edited by Helen Grace, Ghassan Hage, Lesley Johnson, Julie Langsworth, and Michael Symonds. Pluto Press.

Hage, Ghassan. 1998. *White Nation: Fantasies of White Supremacy in a Multicultural Society.* Pluto Press.

Hage, Ghassan. 2012. "Critical Anthropological Thought and the Radical Political Imaginary Today." *Critique of Anthropology* 32 (3): 285–308.

Hage, Ghassan. 2015. *Alter-Politics: Critical Anthropology and the Radical Imagination.* Melbourne University Publishing.

Harrell-Bond, Barbara E. 1986. *Imposing Aid: Emergency Assistance to Refugees.* Oxford University Press.

Harrell-Bond, Barbara E. 1999. "The Experience of Refugees as Recipients of Aid." In *Refugees: Perspectives on the Experience of Forced Migration*, edited by Alastair Ager. Pinter.

Harrell-Bond, Barbara E., and Eftihia Voutira. 1992. "Anthropology and the Study of Refugees." *Anthropology Today* 8 (4): 6–10.

Heidegger, Martin. 1962. *Being and Time.* Translated by John Macquarrie and Edward S. Robinson. Harper & Row.

Heidegger, Martin. 1971. *Poetry, Language, Thought.* Translated by Albert Hofstadter. Harper and Row.

Herlihy, Jane, Peter Scragg, and Stuart Turner. 2002. "Discrepancies in Autobiographical Memories—Implications for the Assessment of Asylum Seekers: Repeated Interviews Study." *British Medical Journal* 324 (7333): 324–27.

Herlihy, Jane, and Stuart W. Turner. 2007. "Asylum Claims and Memory of Trauma: Sharing Our Knowledge." *British Journal of Psychiatry* 191 (1): 3–4.

Hobsbawm, Eric. 1990. *Nations and Nationalism Since 1780: Programme, Myth, Reality.* Cambridge University Press.

Hoffstaedter, Gerhard. 2011a. *Modern Muslim Identities: Negotiating Religion and Ethnicity in Malaysia.* NIAS Press.

Hoffstaedter, Gerhard. 2011b. "Radical Othering: Refugees, Displacement and Landscapes of Difference in Malaysia." *The Annual Conference of the Australian Sociological Association (TASA)*, Newcastle, NSW, Australia.

Hoffstaedter, Gerhard. 2013. "Islam and Freedom of Religion: Anthropology, Theology and Clashes of Universalisms in Contemporary Malaysia." *The Australian Journal of Anthropology* 24 (3): 270–89.

Hoffstaedter, Gerhard. 2014a. "Working For (Bare) Life: Refugees in the Concrete Jungle." *Griffith Review* 45: 117–24.

Hoffstaedter, Gerhard. 2014b. "Place-Making: Chin Refugees, Citizenship and the State in Malaysia." *Citizenship Studies* 18 (8): 871–84.

Hoffstaedter, Gerhard. 2015. "Urban Refugees and the UNHCR in Kuala Lumpur: Dependency, Assistance and Survival." In *Urban Refugees: Challenges in Protection, Services and Policy*, edited by Gerhard Hoffstaedter and Koichi Koizumi. Routledge.

Hoffstaedter, Gerhard. 2016. "The Limits of Compassion." *Overland* 224: 69–74.

Hoffstaedter, Gerhard. 2017a. "The Dominant Discourses of Refugees, Recognition, and Othering in Malaysia." *Situations: Cultural Studies in the Asian Context* 10 (2): 27–44.

Hoffstaedter, Gerhard. 2017b. "Refugees, Islam, and the State: The Role of Religion in Providing Sanctuary in Malaysia." *Journal of Immigrant & Refugee Studies* 15 (3): 287–304.

Hoffstaedter, Gerhard. 2020. "Rohingya People." In *SAGE Encyclopedia of the Sociology of Religion*, edited by Adam Possamai and Anthony J. Blasi. Sage.

Hoffstaedter, Gerhard. 2023. "People Smuggling in Southeast Asia: Rohingya and Chin Stories of Agency, Freedom, and Power in Cross-Border Movement." In *Global Human Smuggling: Buying Freedom in a Retreating World*, edited by Luigi Achilli and David Kyle. Johns Hopkins University Press.

Hoffstaedter, Gerhard. and Aslam Abd Jalil. 2025. "The (Un)official Refugee Protection Regimes in Malaysia: What Is the Way Forward?" In *Refugee Protection in Southeast Asia: Between Humanitarianism and Sovereignty,* edited by Susan Kneebone, Reyvi Mariñas, Antje Missbach, and Max Walden. Berghahn.

Hoffstaedter, Gerhard, and Nicole Lamb. 2019. "It's God's Plan to Be Here": Displacement, Transit and Resettlement of Chin and Karenni Refugees to Australia. *Australian Journal of Politics & History* 65 (4): 584–99.

Hoffstaedter, Gerhard, and Antje Missbach. 2021. "Facilitating Irregular Migration Into Malaysia and From Indonesia: Illicit Markets, Endemic Corruption and Symbolic Attempts to Overcome Impunity." *Public Anthropologist* 3 (1): 8–31.

Hoffstaedter, Gerhard. and Missbach, Antje. 2022. "Graves Beyond the Waves: Survival, Strandedness and Deferred Place-Making in Non-Places in the Andaman Sea." *Journal of Ethnic and Migration Studies* 50 (8): 2063–2077.

Holston, James. 1999. *Cities and Citizenship*. Duke University Press.

Howard, John. 2001. "John Howard: Speech." October 28. https://electionspeeches.moadoph.gov.au/speeches/2001-john-howard.

Human Rights Watch. 2000. "Burmese Refugees in Bangladesh: Still No Durable Solution." Vol. 12, No. 3 (C). May.

Humphrey, Caroline. 2004. "Sovereignty." In *A Companion to the Anthropology of Politics*, edited by David Nugent and Joan Vincent. Blackwell Publishing.

Inghilleri, Moira. 2005. "Mediating Zones of Uncertainty: Interpreter Agency, the Interpreting Habitus and Political Asylum Adjudication." *The Translator* 11 (1): 69–85.

Isin, Engin F. 2002. *Being Political: Genealogies of Citizenship*. University of Minnesota Press.

Isin, Engin F. 2008. "Theorizing Acts of Citizenship." In *Acts of Citizenship*, edited by Engin F. Isin and Greg M. Nielsen. Zed Books.

Jackson, Michael. 2002. *The Politics of Storytelling: Violence, Transgression and Intersubjectivity*. Museum Tusculanum Press.

Jacobsen, Karen. 2005. *The Economic Life of Refugees*. Kumarian Press.

Jalil, Aslam Abd. 2023. "The Right to Work for Refugees in Malaysia: Protection, Livelihoods, and Dignity." PhD thesis, School of Social Science, University of Queensland.

Jalil, Aslam Abd, and Gerhard Hoffstaedter. 2023. "The Effects of COVID-19 on Refugees in Peninsular Malaysia: Surveillance, Securitisation and Eviction." *Advances in Southeast Asian Studies* 16(1): 79–99.

Jalil, Aslam Abd, and Gerhard Hoffstaedter. 2024. "Refugee Registration Schemes in Malaysia: Governing Refugees by Retaining the Status Quo and Reinforcing Borders." *Migration and Society* 7 (1): 46–61.

Jansen, Bram J. 2008. "Between Vulnerability and Assertiveness: Negotiating Resettlement in Kakuma Refugee Camp, Kenya." *African Affairs* 107 (429): 569–87.

Jaspers, Karl. 1967. *Philosophische Aufsätze*. Frankfurt am Main: Fischer Bücherei.

Johnston, Michael. 2005. *Syndromes of Corruption: Wealth, Power, and Democracy*. Cambridge University Press.

Kagan, Michael. 2003. "Is Truth in the Eye of the Beholder? Objective Credibility Assessment in Refugee Status Determination." *Georgetown Immigration Law Journal* 17 (3): 367–415.

Kahn, Joel S. 2006. *Other Malays: Nationalism and Cosmopolitanism in the Modern Malay World*. Singapore University Press.

Kaiser, Tania. 2005. "Participating in Development? Refugee Protection, Politics and Developmental Approaches to Refugee Management in Uganda." *Third World Quarterly* 26 (2): 351–67.

Karčić, Hamza. 2014. "One-Way Ticket to Kuala Lumpur." *Indonesia and the Malay World* 42 (124): 400–17.

Kibreab, Gaim. 2004. "Pulling the Wool Over the Eyes of the Strangers: Refugee Deceit and Trickery in Institutionalized Settings." *Journal of Refugee Studies* 17 (1): 1–26.

Kinnvall, Catarina. 2004. "Globalization and Religious Nationalism: Self, Identity, and the Search for Ontological Security." *Political Psychology* 25 (5): 741–67.

Kleist, Nauja, and Stef Jansen. 2016. "Introduction: Hope Over Time: Crisis, Immobility and Future-Making." *History and Anthropology* 27 (4): 373–92.

Kneebone, Susan. 2010. "The Governance of Labor Migration in Southeast Asia." *Global Governance* 16 (3): 383–96.

Laing, Ronald D. 1960. *The Divided Self: An Existential Study in Sanity and Madness*. Tavistock.

Lamb, Nicole, and Gerhard Hoffstaedter. 2020. "'We Walk, We Laugh, We Dance': Refugee Experiences of Older Chin Women in Kuala Lumpur." *Ageing and Society* 40 (5): 1021–1038.

Lehman, F. K. 1963. *The Structure of Chin Society: A Tribal People of Burma Adapted to a Non-Western Civilization*. University of Illinois Press.

Liow, Joseph Chinyong. 2009. *Piety and Politics: Islamism in Contemporary Malaysia*. Oxford University Press.

Long, Katy. 2013. *The Point of No Return: Refugees, Rights, and Repatriation*. Oxford University Press.

Malkki, Liisa. H. 1995a. *Purity and Exile: Violence, Memory, and National Cosmology among Hutu Refugees in Tanzania*. University of Chicago Press.

Malkki, Liisa H. 1995b. "Refugees and Exile: From 'Refugee Studies' to the National Order of Things." *Annual Review of Anthropology* 24 (1): 495–523.

Malpas, Jeff. 2006. *Heidegger's Topology: Being, Place, World*. MIT Press.

Mang, K. 2011. *Burmanisation and Religious Persecution in Chin State*. Chin Human Rights Organization.

Maryns, Katrijn. 2006. *The Asylum Speaker: Language in the Belgian Asylum Procedure*. St. Jerome Publishing.

Mauss, Marcel. (1954) 2002. *The Gift: The Form and Reason for Exchange in Archaic Societies*. Translated by W. D. Halls. Routledge.

Mayberry, Kate. 2015. "First-Class Refugees: Malaysia's Two-Tier System." *Al-Jazeera*. December 27. http://www.aljazeera.com/indepth/features/2015/12/class-refugees-malaysia-tier-system-151221061627431.html.

McConnachie, Kirsten. 2018. "Securitization and Community-Based Protection Among Chin Refugees in Kuala Lumpur." *Social & Legal Studies* 28 (2): 158–78.

Mehta, Suketu. 2011. "The Asylum Seeker." *The New Yorker*. July 25.

Menon, Praveen. 2015. "Malaysia Finds 139 Graves in 'Cruel' Jungle Trafficking Camps." Reuters. May 25. Accessed November 1, 2025. http://www.reuters.com/article/us-asia-migrants-idUSKBN0OA06W20150525.

Miéville, China. 2009. *The City & the City*. Del Rey Ballantine Books.

Mitzen, Jennifer. 2006. "Ontological Security in World Politics: State Identity and the Security Dilemma." *European Journal of International Relations* 12 (3): 341–70.

Mohajan, Haradhan Kumar. 2018. "History of Rakhine State and the Origin of the Rohingya Muslims." *Indonesian Journal of Social Sciences* 10 (1): 177–88.

Morin, Edgar, and Anne Brigitte Kern. 1999. *Homeland Earth: A Manifesto for the New Millennium*. Hampton Press.

Muniandy, Parthiban. 2021. *Ghost Lives of the Pendatang: Informality and Cosmopolitan Contaminations in Urban Malaysia*. Palgrave Macmillan Singapore.

Munro, Jenny, and Gerhard Hoffstaedter. 2020. "COVID-19 and 'Medical Citizenship': How the Pandemic Is Generating New Forms of Belonging and Exclusion." *ABC Religion and Ethics*. June 22. https://www.abc.net.au/religion/coronavirus-and-medical-citizenship/12379794.

Nah, Alice M. 2007. Struggling with (Il)legality: The Indeterminate Functioning of Malaysia's Borders for Asylum Seekers, Refugees, and Stateless Persons. In *Borderscapes: Hidden Geographies and Politics at Territory's Edge*, edited by Prem Kumar Rajaram and Carl Grundy-Warr. University of Minnesota Press.

Nah, Alice M. 2010. "Refugees and Space in Urban Areas in Malaysia." *Forced Migration Review* 34: 29–31.

Nail, Thomas. 2015. *The Figure of the Migrant*. Stanford University Press.

Othman, Norani, Mavis Puthucheary, and Clive Kessler, eds. 2008. *Sharing the Nation: Faith, Difference, Power and the State 50 Years After Merdeka*. Strategic Information and Research Development Centre.

Nyers, Peter. 2006. *Rethinking Refugees: Beyond States of Emergency*. Routledge.

O'Brien, Melanie, and Gerhard Hoffstaedter. 2020. "'There We Are Nothing, Here We Are Nothing!'—The Enduring Effects of Rohingya Persecution and Genocide in Myanmar on Their Lives in the Diaspora." *Social Sciences* 9 (11): 209–16.

Ong, Aihwa. 2006. *Neoliberalism as Exception: Mutations in Citizenship and Sovereignty*. Duke University Press.

Organisation of Islamic Cooperation. 1990. "Cairo Declaration on Human Rights in Islam." https://digitallibrary.un.org/record/113201?ln=en&v=pdf.

Othman, Norani, Mavis Puthucheary, and Clive S. Kessler. "Introduction: A Shared Nation." In *Sharing the Nation: Faith, Difference, Power and the State 50 Years After Merdeka*, edited by Norani Othman, Mavis Puthucheary, and Clive S. Kessler. Strategic Information and Research Development Centre.

Owens, Patricia. 2010. "Reclaiming 'Bare Life'?: Against Agamben on Refugees." *International Relations* 23 (4): 567–82.

Palmer, Catherine. 2009. "Soccer and the Politics of Identity for Young Muslim Refugee Women in South Australia." *Soccer & Society* 10 (1): 27–38.

Patrick, Peter L. 2012. "Language Analysis for Determination of Origin: Objective Evidence for Refugee Status Determination." In *The Oxford Handbook of Language and Law*, edited by Peter M. Tiersma and Lawrence M. Solan. Oxford University Press.

Pöllabauer, Sonja. 2004. "Interpreting in Asylum Hearings: Issues of Role, Responsibility and Power." *Interpreting* 6 (2): 143–80.

Preston, Rosemary. 1991. "The Provision of Education to Refugees in Places of Temporary Asylum: Some Implications for Development." *Comparative Education* 27 (1): 61–81.

Price, Richard. 1990. *Alabi's World*. Johns Hopkins University Press.

Price, Richard. 1996. *Maroon Societies: Rebel Slave Communities in the Americas*. 3rd ed. Johns Hopkins University Press.

Price, Richard. 2005. Executing Ethnicity: The Killings in Suriname. *Cultural Anthropology* 20 (4): 437–71.

Puthucheary, Mavis. 2008. "Malaysia's Social Contract: The Invention and Historical Evolution of an Idea." In *Sharing the Nation: Faith, Difference, Power and the State 50 Years After Merdeka*, edited by Norani Othman, Mavis Puthucheary, and Clive S. Kessler. Strategic Information and Research Development Centre.

Putnam, Robert D. 2000. *Bowling Alone: The Collapse and Revival of American Community*. Simon & Schuster.

Rajaram, Prem Kumar, and Grundy-Warr, Carl, eds. 2007. *Borderscapes: Hidden Geographies and Politics at Territory's Edge*. University of Minnesota Press.

Ramalingam, Chithra Latha. 2011. "Globalization of Sports: A Solution for Multiculturalism in Malaysia." *Jati—Journal of Southeast Asian Studies* 16 (1): 233–49.

Refugees International. 2009. *Stateless Again: Palestinian-Origin Refugees From Iraq*. Refugees International.

Reno, William. 1995. *Corruption and State Politics in Sierra Leone*. Cambridge University Press.

Richards, Adam, Parveen Parmar, and Richard Sollom. 2011. *Life Under the Junta: Evidence of Crimes Against Humanity in Burma's Chin State*. Physicians for Human Rights.

Richmond, Anthony H. 1994. *Global Apartheid: Refugees, Racism, and the New World Order*. Oxford University Press.

Riva, Sara, and Gerhard Hoffstaedter. 2021. "The Aporia of Refugee Rights in a Time of Crises: The Role of Brokers in Accessing Refugee Protection in Transit and at the Border." *Comparative Migration Studies* 9 (1). https://doi.org/10.1186/s40878-020-00212-2.

Rogers, Hannah, Simone Fox, and Jane Herlihy. 2015. "The Importance of Looking Credible: The Impact of the Behavioural Sequelae of Post-Traumatic Stress Disorder on the Credibility of Asylum Seekers." *Psychology, Crime & Law* 21 (2): 139–55. https://doi.org/10.1080/1068316X.2014.951643

Roitman, Janet. 2021. "Framing the Crisis: COVID-19." August 30. https://ssrn.com/abstract=3952226.

Rosaldo, Renato. 1997. "Cultural Citizenship, Inequality, and Multiculturalism." In *Latino Cultural Citizenship*, edited by William V. Flores and Rina Benmayor. Beacon Press.

Rose-Ackerman, Susan. 1999. *Corruption and Government: Causes, Consequences, and Reform*. Cambridge University Press.

Rozakou, Katerina. 2015. "The Biopolitics of Hospitality in Greece: Humanitarianism and the Management of Refugees." *American Ethnologist* 42 (3): 562–77.

Sakhong, Lian Hmung. 2003. *In Search of Chin Identity: A Study in Religion, Politics and Ethnic Identity in Burma*. NIAS Press.

Sakhong, Lian Hmung. 2012. *The Dynamics of Sixty Years of Ethnic Armed Conflict in Burma*. Burma Center Prague.

Sanford, Victoria, and Asale Angel-Ajani. 2006. *Engaged Observer: Anthropology, Advocacy, and Activism*. Rutgers University Press.

Schinkel, Willem. 2013. "The Imagination of 'Society' in Measurements of Immigrant Integration." *Ethnic and Racial Studies* 36 (7): 1142–161.

Scott, James C. 1985. *Weapons of the Weak: Everyday Forms of Peasant Resistance*. Yale University Press.

Scott, James C. 1998. *Seeing Like a State: How Certain Schemes to Improve the Human Condition Have Failed*. Yale University Press.

Shan Human Rights Foundation. 2002. *Charcoal and Pork: Shan State under the SPDC.* SHRF.

Sigona, Nando. 2012. "'I Have Too Much Baggage': The Impacts of Legal Status on the Social Worlds of Irregular Migrants." *Social Anthropology* 20 (1): 50–65.

Sigona, Nando. 2014. "The Politics of Refugee Voices: Representations, Narratives, and Memories." In *The Oxford Handbook of Refugee and Forced Migration Studies*, edited by Elena Fiddian-Qasmiyeh, Gil Loescher, Katy Long, and Nando Sigona. Oxford University Press.

Smith, Matthew, and Taylor Landis. 2014. *Policies of Persecution: Ending Abusive State Policies against Rohingya Muslims in Myanmar*. Fortify Rights. February. https://www.fortifyrights.org/downloads/Policies_of_Persecution_Feb_25_Fortify_Rights.pdf.

Spaaij, Ramon F. J. 2011. *Sport and Social Mobility: Crossing Boundaries.* Routledge.

Spaaij, Ramón. 2012. "Beyond the Playing Field: Experiences of Sport, Social Capital and Integration Among Somalis in Australia." *Ethnic and Racial Studies* 35 (9): 1519–538.

Spaaij, Ramón. 2015. "Refugee Youth, Belonging and Community Sport." *Leisure Studies* 34 (3): 303–18.

Sweeney, James A. 2009. "Credibility, Proof and Refugee Law." *International Journal of Refugee Law* 21 (4): 700–26.

Szeftel, Morris. 1998. "Misunderstanding African Politics: Corruption and the Governance Agenda." *Review of African Political Economy* 25(76): 221–40.

Thomas, Robert. 2006. "Assessing the Credibility of Asylum Claims: EU and UK Approaches Examined." *European Journal of Migration and Law*, 8(1), 79–96.

Tooze, Adam. 2022. "Welcome to the World of the Polycrisis." *Financial Times*, October 28.

Turner, Simon. 2016. "What Is a Refugee Camp? Explorations of the Limits and Effects of the Camp." *Journal of Refugee Studies* 29 (2): 139–48.

Turton, David. 2005. "The Meaning of Place in a World of Movement: Lessons From Long-Term Field Research in Southern Ethiopia." *Journal of Refugee Studies* 18 (3): 258–80.

UN DESA (United Nations Department of Economic and Social Affairs, Population Division). 2019a. *World Population Prospects 2019: Highlights*. https://population.un.org/wpp/assets/Files/WPP2019_Highlights.pdf.

UN DESA (United Nations Department of Economic and Social Affairs, Population Division). 2019b. *International Migrant Stock 2019*. https://www.un.org/development/desa/pd/content/international-migrant-stock.

UN DESA (United Nations Department of Economic and Social Affairs, Population Division). 2024. *World Population Prospects 2024*. Accessed July 10, 2026. https://population.un.org/wpp/.

UNHCR (United Nations High Commissioner for Refugees). 2013. *Beyond Proof: Credibility Assessment in EU Asylum Systems*.

UNHCR (United Nations High Commissioner for Refugees). 2023. *Global Trends: Forced Displacement in 2022*.

UNHCR (United Nations High Commissioner for Refugees). 2026a. *Global Trends: Forced Displacement in 2025*. Accessed July 10, 2026. https://www.unhcr.org/global-trends.

UNHCR (United Nations High Commissioner for Refugees). 2026b. "Figures at a Glance." Accessed July 10, 2026. https://www.unhcr.org/about-unhcr/overview/figures-glance.

UNHCR Malaysia. 2025. "Figures at a Glance: Malaysia." https://www.unhcr.org/my/what-we-do/figures-glance-malaysia.

Van Houtum, Henk, and Ton Van Naerssen. 2002. "Bordering, Ordering and Othering." *Tijdschrift voor economische en sociale geografie* 93 (2): 125–36.

Vigh, Henrik. 2009. "Motion Squared: A Second Look at the Concept of Social Navigation." *Anthropological Theory* 9 (4): 419–38.

Wake, Caitlin, and Tania Cheung. 2016. "Livelihood Strategies of Rohingya Refugees in Malaysia: 'We Want to Live in Dignity'." Humanitarian Policy Group Working Paper. June. Overseas Development Institute.

Wake, Caitlin, and Yu, Brenda. 2018. "The Rohingya Crisis: Making The Transition From Emergency To Longer-Term Development." Policy Brief 71. March. Overseas Development Institute.

Walseth, Kristin. 2008. "Bridging and Bonding Social Capital in Sport—Experiences of Young Women With an Immigrant Background." *Sport, Education and Society* 13 (1): 1–17.

Wan Syamsul Amly. 2015. "Zakat Rohingya: 'Ramai lagi rakyat kita yang susah'—Che Mat" [Zakat Rohingya: 'Many more of our people are in difficulty'—Che Mat]. *Astro Awani*. http://www.astroawani.com/berita-malaysia/zakat-rohingya-ramai-lagi-rakyat-kita-yang-susah-che-mat-61390.

Whitaker, Beth Elise. 2002. "Refugees in Western Tanzania: The Distribution of Burdens and Benefits Among Local Hosts." *Journal of Refugee Studies* 15 (4): 339–58.

Wimmer, Andreas. 2008. "The Making and Unmaking of Ethnic Boundaries: A Multilevel Process Theory." *American Journal of Sociology* 113 (4): 970–1022.

Young, Julian. 2002. *Heidegger's Later Philosophy*. Cambridge University Press.

Zarni, Maung, and Alice Cowley. 2014. "The Slow-Burning Genocide of Myanmar's Rohingya." *Pacific Rim Law & Policy Journal* 23 (3): 683–754.

Zetter, Roger. 2007. "More Labels, Fewer Refugees: Remaking the Refugee Label in an Era of Globalization." *Journal of Refugee Studies* 20 (2): 172–92.

Zetter, Roger. 2014. *Protecting Forced Migrants: A State of the Art Report of Concepts, Challenges and Ways Forward.* Swiss Federal Commission on Migration (FCM).

Index

D

Q

R

Z

The authorized representative in the EU for product safety and compliance is:
Mare Nostrum Group
B.V Doelen 72
4831 GR Breda
The Netherlands

www.ingramcontent.com/pod-product-compliance
Lightning Source LLC
LaVergne TN
LVHW090923220826
846271LV00023B/78
* 9 7 8 1 9 3 1 3 6 8 7 6 6 *